THE FINANCIAL SIDE
OF INDUSTRIAL
RESEARCH MANAGEMENT

THE FINANCIAL SIDE
OF INDUSTRIAL
RESEARCH MANAGEMENT

LYNN W. ELLIS

A Wiley-Interscience Publication
JOHN WILEY & SONS
New York • Chichester • Brisbane • Toronto • Singapore

Copyright © 1984 by John Wiley & Sons, Inc.

All rights reserved. Published simultaneously in Canada.

Reproduction or translation of any part of this work
beyond that permitted by Section 107 or 108 of the
1976 United States Copyright Act without the permission
of the copyright owner is unlawful. Requests for
permission or further information should be addressed to
the Permissions Department, John Wiley & Sons, Inc.

Library of Congress Cataloging in Publication Data:

Ellis, Lynn W. (Lynn Webster), 1928–
  The financial side of industrial research management.

  "A Wiley-Interscience publication."
  Includes bibliographical references and index.
  1. Research, Industrial—Finance.   I. Title.

HD30.4.E44   1984   658.5'7'0681   83-19658
ISBN 0-471-89056-1

Printed in the United States of America

10 9 8 7 6 5 4 3 2 1

To Eileen
Editor, Grammarian, and Critic

PREFACE

Every professional manager has three job-related facets to his or her work, and the industrial research manager is no exception. First there is the need to be a manager of people. Not only are there tasks to administer, but also there is the further need to build a team with a unity of purpose and a mix of generalist and specialist skills to make the whole more effective than the sum of the parts. Almost the whole of engineering management literature is built around this aspect of the research manager's job.

The second facet is the external part of the job. Not only must the industrial research manager be an interface to other functions in the firm, but he or she must also represent the firm in the technological and scientific community at large. Equally, the research department must draw on that community for knowledge so that the work of the team is not wasted on reinventing the wheel.

This book is not based on these first two tasks of the research manager, but rather on the third task, which is economic, entrepreneurial, and financial. The industrial research manager is part of an economic system that measures its efficacy in terms of money. Except for the limited few who have studied business administration, new research managers are largely novices to this task. It is to this audience, therefore, that this book is addressed to fill a perceived gap in the literature.

This book has been structured to explain *why* and to teach *how*. Many quantitative examples are given that relate to real instances of financial decision making in research and development programs. As such, they involve data which are proprietary to the companies from which they were derived. Accordingly, items such as calendar years, dollar amounts, and product lines may have been changed to protect their proprietary nature. On the other hand, the various financial ratios (such as internal rate of return) reflect actual projects as do the trend lines on graphs derived from these ratios.

An attempt has been made to make this book suitable for both self-teaching and classroom work. When used for the latter, and as a supplement to the former, it would be appropriate to augment this book's material with case studies. A few of these have been noted, but many more are being written each year, and a current listing of those available should be sought.

In the industrial sector, the terms *research, applied research, technology,* and *product* or *process development* are used in different ways in different companies. But all are part of the same task to prepare for change in the firm, and differ only in their relevant time horizons. Present financial accounting standards call only for reporting research and development (R&D) as a combined total. For these reasons, all of these terms are used relatively interchangeably in this book, and the principles delineated are equally adequate for the full range from pioneering work to day-to-day development, when due allowance is made for the time value of money.

Finally, it was not the author's intent in writing this book to slight research management in the public sector where so much of current research is undertaken. However, the industrial research manager lives not only by the signs of people and mathematics, but also by the dollar sign. Because of this need to live in a financially-oriented world, this book is principally addressed to the manager in industry, with a brief discourse in the penultimate chapter on how the lessons expounded relate to the task of the public-sector research manager.

While the experience on which this book is based is drawn from more than 35 years of work in industry, the conclusions, errors, and omissions are my own and do not necessarily reflect the views of any past or present employers.

LYNN W. ELLIS

Westport, Connecticut
November 1983

CONTENTS

THE FINANCIAL SIDE
OF INDUSTRIAL
RESEARCH MANAGEMENT

1

THE ECONOMIC
TASK OF THE
RESEARCH MANAGER

Writers on long-range planning have for years stressed the need to look at a business in its entirety and to provide an appropriate structure for making decisions within this context (Drucker, 1959). The reason is that decisions are not the individual, isolated acts of various functional managers; each decision affects the whole business and the tasks of other departments.

The economic task of the industrial research manager is inextricably linked to the economic needs of the business firm. Only when one fully understands the strategy and objectives of the entire business can a course of action be set for the industrial research department. In the process, one must organize to work with other business functions, as well as to compete with them for a proper share of scarce resources. Thus, understanding the economic task of R&D begins with a knowledge of the economic task of the firm.

THE ECONOMIC TASK OF THE FIRM

For a technically trained individual, it is rational to study the economic dimension of industrial activity as a multiloop linked system, as depicted graphically in Figure 1.1. A number of authors have looked at such systems in depth (Boulding, 1956; Weinberg, 1975).

The general system in this case is the national (or international) economy at the macrolevel. The economy consists of a number of specific microlevel systems representing individual corporations, government bodies, and educational and scientific organizations. Within all but the most narrowly focused corporations, operations are carried out by specific businesses which are also systems.

The Operating Task of a Line of Business

Within the specific system that is an individual line of business headed by a general manager, there are a number of individual subsystems that relate to each other, to general management, and to specific systems outside the firm. With today's multiproduct (conglomerate) industrial organizations, there may be also another systems layer above the level of business system, but it is at the business level where cohesive analysis and modeling must be done.

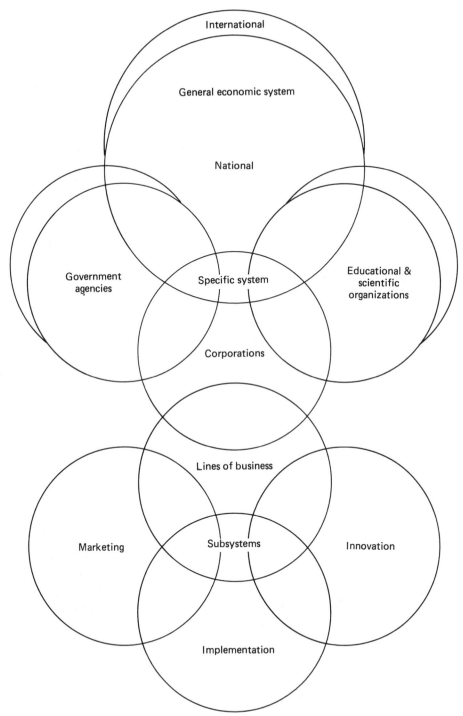

Figure 1.1. Systems in industrial activity

3

The PIMS (profit impact of market strategies) study has (since 1972) looked at thousands of diverse businesses in hundreds of corporations seeking to establish relationships between profit performance and selected aspects of strategic planning (Schoeffler et al, 1974). This study sought to identify the factors influencing profitability in a line of business, quantify them, and interpret how return on investment (ROI) changes in response to strategic allocations of various resources such as capital, marketing, and R&D expense.

An early conclusion concerning R&D spending was that it interacts strongly with market share, although the positive correlation does not necessarily indicate causation. With high market share, profitability (ROI) was highest when R&D spending was highest, whereas the inverse was true with low market share. Low ROI would tend to lead to business decisions curtailing R&D activities, but whether the higher margins are the profitable consequence, or the cause, of increasing R&D was not shown by the PIMS model (more of this cause and effect relation is covered in Chapter 8).

A more recent report on the PIMS study (Strategic Planning Institute, 1977) shows other interactions between R&D and other corporate sectors. One in particular is that high R&D spending and high marketing spending are disasterous for ROI.

For the purpose of understanding the task of the research manager, the number of operating subsystems discussed will be limited to three (marketing, implementation, and innovation) with the remainder subsumed in general management. Internally, all subsystems have direct relations with the others.

Marketing Subsystem.   Externally, marketing's task—to satisfy customers—is related to other specific systems in the general economy. To achieve customer satisfaction, marketing must identify the customers' perceptions of value and relate them to the research manager for incorporation in new products. Because so many research managers express dissatisfaction with this information channel, some further explanation of the marketing subsystem is required.

Much of marketing is done through indirect channels. Consumer products flow through wholesalers and retailers to the end customer. Industrial parts flow to the end users through distributors and/or original equipment manufacturers and their distributors. Suppliers of public utilities can use their clients' organizations to reach the ultimate customer. Thus, in practice a firm's marketing department has multiple customers: the end user and one or more distributing customers who may attenuate and distort the end user's values when communicating them to the supplier. Typically, consumer products marketing departments test the end user indirectly. Often other marketing departments do not, resulting in an imperfect flow of information.

Implementation Subsystem. The implementation subsystem of a business is charged with providing its economic goods or services. These include manufacturing, installation, distribution, or field service according to the character of the business. The implementation subsystem is connected externally through the marketing functions quantification of customer needs and through a strong direct external interface via its purchasing department to its material suppliers. The research manager must respect and work with this external interface to be successful with internal interfaces with the implementation function.

Innovation Subsystem. The last major function is innovation, defined as the successful economic introduction of change into the marketplace. This subsystem, broader than the research and development function, takes in the product planning function of marketing and the production/process planning function of implementation, usually identified as industrial engineering. In addition, this subsystem needs a broad external interface to the specific scientific and technological systems of the general economy.

Alpha Electrical Industries Limited (not its real name) is an old-line telephone and electrical products company in Europe, founded before the turn of the century. Of its several divisions, two in particular illustrate the nature of innovation.

The largest division in the company, with proportionally the greatest share of total net income, is the telephone switching division, which makes the central office equipment that sets up telephone calls in response to the digits dialed by subscribers. From the company's inception to the mid-1960s, this equipment was electromechanical, with high tooling costs, specialized production machinery, and long product life cycles. This situation created substantial manufacturing economies of scale (Ellis, 1979). Thus, only some twenty competitors in the industrialized world had, like Alpha, the competence and resources to introduce new generations of switching equipment.

One of the medium-sized divisions is the telecommunications transmission equipment division, which manufactures the long-distance specialized equipment used to connect together telephone central offices in different cities. From its earliest days it was an innovator in electronics, from vacuum tubes to transistors to integrated circuits. Economies of scale in manufacturing count for much less in this type of equipment, which uses electronic components that are widely available from other suppliers. Thus, the division has several times as many worldwide competitors as the telephone switching division, and its management is correspondingly attuned to change.

In the mid-1960s, the evolution in semiconductor-technology called for new generations of products in both divisions. The transmission manager had seen AT&T adopt digital technology for transmission in the United States, and eagerly adapted it to European conditions. To the switching manager, however, such a radical shift was judged more than was necessary in terms of product planning in the marketplace and more than the engineering and manufacturing departments could handle. Alpha opted, therefore, for modern electronics only in the control section of the central offices, replacing relays by a small computer and continuing to use electromechanical relays (of a new type) in the actual switching circuitry. AT&T and most worldwide competitors adopted a parallel course of action. The warnings of impending obsolescence from the switching manager's counterpart went unheeded. New plant investment paralleled R&D expense based on a product life projection through the 1970s.

Two of Alpha's competitors, one French and one Canadian, looked at the discontinuity in the technological system as an opportunity to introduce successful economic change to the marketplace. By the mid-1970s, both had working digital switching systems in service, and Alpha (and almost all of its competitors) were actively developing comparable equipment. The transmission manager became the head of Alpha's merged digital telecommunications division.

The economic consequences to Alpha of the shortened life cycle of its semielectronic switch were extra write-offs of capital and high R&D expenses, because the costs of completing the engineering of this switch overlapped the development of a digital one. By the tme the latter entered production, the implementation function had radically altered, with fewer workers doing totally different assembly operations and with computerized testing. The lesson learned was that technological innovation requires radical change in human behavior.

A business organization is one of the few human structures organized to provide purposeful change in response to changing technology. Indeed, most manufacturers cannot live without new products and it is common for over half of current sales to come from products introduced in the previous decade (Booz-Allen, 1975). In the United States, industrial research and development expenditures have increased from one-tenth of a percent 50 years ago to a composite average of 2% of sales in 1980 and 1981 (*Business Week*, July 5, 1982, p. 54).

The economic operating task of the firm can then be defined as organizing to work through its internal subsystems of management, marketing, implementation, and innovation, and the external environmental interfaces of the latter three with customers, suppliers, and technological evolution, respectively, to supply an economic good or service. By *economic* is meant a level of profitability sufficiently large to compensate for the risk inherent in the selected business strategy.

The process of strategic planning is an essential element in gaining control of R&D, for R&D targets are only one portion of the encompassing objective of achieving a competitive position. The relationship of external and internal factors is paramount for joining the opportunities offered by technology to the objectives of the business as a whole. While primarily responsible for the former, the research manager must fit in with and participate in the formulation of the latter.

The Financial Management Task of the Firm

Good management requires that the operating and financing tasks be considered separately. Since research management is an operating function, it may seem strange to raise the issue of financing the firm, but there is a relationship that will be developed here briefly and extended in future chapters.

The essence of the relationship is that research and development is really an investment. That is, it is an outlay of cash today in the expectation of profit in an uncertain tomorrow. Further, it commits the business to a course of action limiting the scope of future decisions just as much as does an investment in plant and equipment.

An excellent example is the Communications Satellite Corporation in its initial decade (Snow, 1976). Formed following an act of the Congress, Comsat's initial focus was on developing geostationary communications satellites only for international communications, as the designated U.S. participant in the Intelsat Consortium. Engineers of Comsat Laboratories, reinforced by others from other consortium countries, developed and launched five series of satellites in 10 years, raising per satellite capacity from 240 to 6250 two-way circuits in the process. This integration of initial business objective and R&D focus led to capital investment in new satellite facilities at just over 2-year intervals, even before the life of previous series had expired, to take advantage of the greatly reduced per circuit costs of the new designs. Driven by its technology focus, the satellite portion of the Intelsat system invested over $680 million in 10 years. While the company has since added other lines of satellite business through its Comsat General subsidiary, its international business retains its fundamental character from its initial years.

The accounting profession requires that research and development be treated as an expense (FASB 2). Thus, all expenditures for R&D must normally be written off in the time period in which they are incurred. To treat R&D as an operating expense is to minimize it, as some operating managers do. But since R&D is really an investment, it should be considered from a decision-making viewpoint according to financial management precepts.

The tasks of financial management are first to invest wisely, second to raise money economically, and third to set a dividend policy. In investing, there is a cash outlay today and in the near future, in the expectation of a profit over a number of years at a later date. Prudent investment requires that the excess of profits over expenditures be maximized with both values discounted to the present.

The nature of his task obliges the financial manager to a portfolio. For him, investing in innovation is only one of several alternative ways to use money to make a profit (Wood, 1975). The same money could be used to invest in fixed assets (plant and equipment), real estate, or other tangibles which receive capital accounting treatment, or in advertising, market development, or organizational development, which like research are really investments, although they too receive accounting treatment as expenses.

As a consequence, the research manager must compete for his fair share of the scarce resource called money. This competition for investment financing occurs on a case-by-case basis with all competing proposals being matched with innovation proposals at the time of decision making. The number of research proposals that will be chosen depends not only on their intrinsic merits, but also on the returns available at that time on alternatives. These relative returns will vary from time to time depending on the environment external to the firm.

Beta Global Incorporated is a very financially oriented holding company. It gives its subsidiary managers financial objectives for current and longer-term return without regard to relative growth rate, much as a banker would lend out money. These objectives are expressed in return on funds employed (total capital) before income taxes and interest, so that differences in methods of financing of its subsidiaries are not part of its primary operating objectives for general management.

In the worldwide economic expansion years of the 1960s and early 1970s, the highest returns were from the extension of plants, so capital investments secured priority in funds allocation. The oil crisis of 1974–1975 had such a negative effect on common stock prices around the world that in the mid-1970s it became more economic to buy up other companies than to build new facilities, and acquisitions took over funds priorities. With the stock market recovery in the late 1970s accompanied by high interest rates, when both acquisitions and new facilities looked less attractive, growth from within via R&D projects received priority in many subsidiaries.

In the second task—raising money economically—the financial manager has the choice of various forms of debt and/or stock equity, plus retained earnings and depreciation. It is not necessary to go into this in detail because only common stock is interrelated with the research manager's task. For the financial manager to raise money economically through the sale of common stock, the price of the stock must be high with respect to its dividend. For this to be possible, modern financial theory holds that the growth rate of the earnings and dividend streams must be high, as a consequence of successful reinvestment of retained earnings (Van Horne, 1974; Quirin, 1967). This theory's reliance on reinvestment in tangible assets is not incompatible with an efficient market's making due allowances for the hidden reinvestment represented by high research expenditures. That the price/earnings ratio of common stock does increase with increasing continuing levels research expenditure is readily verifiable (Gilman, 1978). With appropriate concern for cause and effect the research manager's economic planning can also be interlocked with this second part of the financing task.

THE RESEARCH MANAGER'S FUNCTION

As is true with any manager, the research manager must plan, organize, measure, and control his department. Each of these activities in turn has an economic dimension.

Economic Planning of Research

Although not uniquely responsible for innovation in the firm, the research manager is the lynchpin of the innovation process. As such he is held responsible by the general manager for a major share of success in innovation. The economic planning process for his department starts with obtaining a fundamental understanding of the strategic objectives and technical opportunities of each line of business.

Unfortunately, the downward communication of strategic objectives is often procedural and uninformative: "Hold R&D to the same percentage of sales as last year." Or, "Since this is a harvest type of business, wind down R&D." Or, "This product is the key to our success and should have full R&D support."

Such setting of objectives is often conflicting, as the indicated actions for R&D may run counter to the strategy of the business when analyzed carefully. Worse still, these objectives usually take for granted that the strategic decisions are correct. Managing strategically requires the research manager to be part of the formulation of objectives so that they reflect the opportunities available in the technology and so that the ones selected move the business in the direction the general manager wishes to pursue (Gluck et al., 1976).

Once appropriate strategic objectives have been agreed on, the initial economic planning task of the research manager is to estimate the appropriate R&D budget. How much should a line of business or a company invest in R&D? To invest too little consigns the busi-

The Gamma Products Company was taken over by Beta Global in the mid-1970s and promptly given increasing year by year targets for return on total capital. The general manager was able to estimate quickly that these targets could not be met by operating efficiencies alone. The marketing vice president was equally skeptical that the existing product base could do more than support minimal increases in market share and thus in profits.

The engineering vice president pointed out the potential in the then beginning surge in the use of microprocessors and outlined how they could be applied to increase functionality in and improve the features of certain traditional electrical and mechanical products. Furthermore, he highlighted the potential for electronic networking of these products to produce systems that would enter a new and growing market sector.

After review by all managers, the general manager made the strategic decision to spend more for research and development than in the recent past, despite its short-term impact on return, to position the company with new products and a systems capability that by the late 1970s would place the company nearer its targeted financial objectives.

ness to the low-margin undifferentiated commodity segment of its industry. On the other hand, because of the accounting treatment of R&D expense, investing too much penalizes current profits. Establishing an optimum level of R&D is thus one economic planning task of the research manager.

The R&D manager, however, as custodian of the technological strength of the firm, is responsible for supporting other less technologically strong functions. Specifically, R&D must provide specialists in case detailed engineering and design are required on a customer's order. The marketing function will normally require some assistance in the preparing and/or technically approving complex proposals or in customer negotiations. And the research department has a responsibility to ensure that its past output moves smoothly through the implementation function and out to customers. Thus, the economic plan of the research manager must also include manpower and budgets for all of these additional tasks.

Finally, the economic plan must provide for the appropriate balance between long and short term. In addition to technology and markets, product evolution has a time dimension (Booz-Allen, 1975). Products have a life cycle spanning introduction, growth, maturity, saturation, and decline and must be replaced periodically if the business is to sustain momentum. Thus, the research manager's economic plan must have replacement products in an appropriate time scale, with the right amount in preparatory phases (exploration, screening, and business analysis), in development and testing, and in the launching phase, which includes implementation and sales. And the entire plan must be expressed not only in terms of *what* products, but also in terms of *money:* How much expenditure is justified and can be supported?

In late 1975, the Gamma Products Company's engineering vice president had studied carefully the initial budget proposals with a normal level of R&D expense, as presented in Table 1.1. It was apparent that they did not meet Beta Global's targets in any year, and that if any belt tightening were ordered, the R&D budget could be one of the areas cut. This, however, would reduce growth so much that by 1980 the return would fall further behind target.

To implement the new products and system, R&D proposed to the general manager would take nearly $1 million. If it were possible to implement such a development in a single year, from 1978 on, the accelerated growth would come much closer to Beta's targets. Such a buildup was not practical through normal recruiting, there would be future morale problems in laying off engineers when the project was finished, and the general manager was certain that Beta would disapprove lowering the 1976 pretax return by the full million dollars.

After several tentative calculations, the manager proposed the flat budget scheme shown in Table 1.1. The budget allowed a manageable 30% first-year buildup, with normal personnel attrition offsetting inflation in three subsequent years. This only provided $600,000 of the needed funding, however, so that R&D was forced to defer other longer-range projects to provide the balance. The percentage return for the increment over the normal budget was 30% (calculated by the internal rate of return method) and was approved.

Organizing Financially

Every research manager who has successfully weathered a budget approval session has had the thought, "Now let me organize to accomplish the task my own way." This is of course impossible, not only because of the requirements of accounting, but also because of general management's prerogatives to approve specific product and process decisions, to decide on test marketing and on full-scale com-

Table 1.1. *Gamma Products Company Budgets, 1976–1980*

| | $ millions by year (in current dollars) | | | | | |
	1975	1976	1977	1978	1979	1980
Beta's targets[a]	2	2.6	3.2	4.0	4.5	4.9
Initial budget with normal R&D						
Sales	20	22	24.2	26.6	29	32
Margin[b]	3	3.3	3.7	4.2	4.8	5.3
R&D	1	1.1	1.2	1.3	1.4	1.5
Return[a]	2	2.2	2.5	2.9	3.4	3.8
Budget with major R&D project						
R&D	1	1.4	1.4	1.4	1.4	1.5
Return[a]	2	1.9	2.2	3.0	3.9	4.5
Better (worse) than normal budget	—	(0.3)	(0.3)	0.1	0.5	0.7

Source. Adapted by author from proprietary data.

[a] Return before interest and income tax.

[b] Margin before R&D, interest and income tax.

mercialization, and to decide on product modification after product launch. Organizing the research program financially involves apportioning the budget allocation into subdivisions that permit all of these objectives operationally, while accumulating costs against targets for accounting purposes.

These budget subdivisions go by various names in different industries: projects, cases, and so forth. A useful analogy is to compare

---

The engineering vice president of Gamma found it easiest to organize his program around each functional product that had a microprocessor. This allowed commercial forecasts to be prepared around each saleable unit, while permitting engineers to estimate hardware and software separately for each programmable product.

The systems side of the program was estimated incrementally. That is, the commercial forecasts were based on the added product sales to be handled as part of systems, and the development costs covered the extra line interface units to permit product networking. Thus, all additional costs of systems business were combined into a separate project.

the research department to a job shop in production. Some form of written proposal is required for each job showing estimated costs, estimated benefits (commercial justification), technical and feature specifications, and schedules.

The problem of missing inputs from marketing, technology, or suppliers was mentioned earlier. One of the essential elements of financial organization is the funding of the work necessary to secure these missing inputs so that project proposals can be properly written. A key ingredient is the provision of discretionary funding for feasibility studies.

Organizing financially requires the establishment of a project selection procedure with some analysis of benefits and costs, which to be effective requires the establishment of criteria for the evaluation of projects. Although procedural controls are necessary, it should be remembered that they are not sufficient if strategic objectives are not adequately thought through.

Finally, organizing the research program financially involves establishing some method for rationing funds. The basic creativity of engineers, scientists, and technologists almost always results in a surfeit of proposals—if not, new people should be sought. Thus, the proposals selected must be brought into line with budget allocations by rationing. Since the research department is in competition for funds with other departments, some rationing method will be required to cope with downward shifts in allocations during the budget year if other departments' more profitable programs are accepted by management. The same rationing procedure will be needed to cope with economic downturns.

Measurement and Control

A research department that has had good economic planning and well-thought-through financial organization is easy to measure and control in economic terms. The reason is because each subdivided task has a cost target or can be further subdivided to provide such targets at the section level of a few engineers, scientists, or computer programmers. Also, because the department is job organized, costs can be measured by simple tools such as weekly time cards against which all time spent is recorded by job numbers, and purchase orders by job number for materials used.

Effective measurement requires that overhead accounts be kept to an absolute minimum. Even such activities as assistance to other departments are capable of having cost targets established and job numbers assigned.

Financial control is thus reduced to the straightforward task of comparing the progression of costs against estimates, coupled with the periodic reestimation of costs-to-complete. Feedback of these reports to the project engineers will sharpen their estimating skills and should result in the average of actual costs being close to the average of estimates.

It should be cautioned, however, that estimation is a statistical process, and a skewed one at that. Overestimates are usually small on individual jobs, and underestimates have a distribution with a long tail—a few jobs go way over in cost in even the best-run research departments. The test of good financial control is therefore whether on the average costs fall near estimates.

When a research department shows a pattern of consistent cost and schedule overruns, it usually involves one of three causes. First, cost figures may not be adequately fed back to the level of project engineering doing the estimating. A second potential cause may be that management may not have faced up to the real costs of R&D and may be insisting on imprudently tight estimates. Third, fuzzy objectives may result in inadequate initial planning and organizing and lead to the disease of "creeping elegance" as products are enhanced while being developed.

FINE STRUCTURING THE ECONOMIC TASK

Having now been once through rather broadly what is the economic task of the research manager, it is appropriate to outline for the balance of the book how this task is to be accomplished in some finer detail. A preliminary step, however, is the introduction of some principles of microeconomics, that is the study of economics at the level of the individual firm. These principles form the topic of Chapter 2.

Two themes were highlighted in discussing the economic planning task of the research manager. Setting the total budget to include the costs of engineering and interfacing with other functions is covered in Chapter 3. The economic task of balancing the time dimension of the research program is treated in Chapter 4.

Next, three themes of detailed financial organization and the management of research tasks are expanded in the following chapter. Chapter 5 covers project selection and evaluation according to objective financial criteria. Chapter 6 addresses the modifications to practice required by risk and uncertainty. The remaining managerial functions of measurement and control are more extensively covered in Chapter 7.

Overall financial control is covered in the next two chapters. Chapter 8 addresses various concepts of how much a company should optimally spend on research and development. Approaches to budget rationing follow in Chapter 9.

The concluding two chapters give some reflections on the applicability of the industrial research approach to the public sector (Chapter 10) and a summary of findings, conclusions, and recommendations (Chapter 11).

REFERENCES

Booz-Allen & Hamilton, *Management of New Products,* New York, 1975.

Boulding, Kenneth J., "General Systems Theory—The Skeleton of Science," *Management Science,* **2**(3): 197 (1956).

Business Week, July 5, 1982, 54–74.

Drucker, Peter F., *The Practice of Management,* New York: Harper & Row, 1954.

Drucker, Peter F., "Long Range Planning," *Managment Science,* **5**(3): (1959).

Drucker, Peter F., *Technology, Management & Society,* New York: Harper & Row, 1970.

Drucker, Peter F., *Management: Analysis, Tasks, Strategies,* New York: Harper & Row, 1975.

Ellis, Lynn W., "Economies of Scale in Telephone Switching Systems," *Proceedings INTELCOM '79,* Dedham, MA: Horizon House, 120–123 (1979).

Financial Accounting Standards Board, *Statement of Financial Accounting Standards No. 2, (FASB 2)—Accounting for Research and Development Costs,* Stamford, CT: October, 1974.

Forrester, Jay W., "Industrial Dynamics: A Major Breakthrough for Decision Makers," *Harvard Business Review,* **36**(4): 37 (1978).

Gilman, John J., "Stock Price and Optimum Research Spending," *Research Management,* **21**(1): 34–36 (1978).

Gluck, Fredrick W., Richard N. Foster, and John C. Forbis, "Cure for Strategic Malnutrition," *Harvard Business Review,* **54**(6): 154–165 (1976).

Quirin, G. David, *The Captial Expenditure Decision,* Homewood, IL: Irwin, 1967.

Schoeffler, Sidney, Robert D. Buzzell, and Donald F. Heany, "The Impact of Strategic Planning on Profit Performance," *Harvard Business Review,* **52** (2): 137–145 (1974).

Snow, Marcellus S., *International Satellite Communications*, New York: Praeger, 1976.

Strategic Planning Institute, *The PIMS Program: Selected Findings*, Cambridge, MA, 1977.

Van Horne, James C., *Financial Management and Policy*, Englewood Cliffs, NJ: Prentice-Hall, 1974.

Weinberg, Gerald, *An Introduction to General Systems Thinking*, New York: Wiley, 1975.

Wood, Edward C., *Case Studies on the Process of Technological Innovations in the Economy's Private Sector*, Menlo Park, CA: Stanford Research Institute, 1975.

2

SOME PRINCIPLES
OF MICROECONOMICS

The economic aspects of business affect daily everyone who is a manager, whether general manager or functional unit head. This applies not only to the economics of the country as a whole usually called *macroeconomics*, but also to the economics of each separate company.

Microeconomics is the study of economics at the level of the individual business firm. Some of the principles of microeconomics need to be understood by research managers since they affect not only their decision making, but also the actions of those other departments with which they interface.

THE TIME VALUE OF MONEY

Research decisions always affect costs and benefits at differing future dates. Yet these decisions must be expressed in terms of today's money. With inflation and interest rates high, future benefits must be higher than costs for the expenditure of research and development funds to be worthwhile. The problem for the decision maker is to determine how much higher they must be to make the decision favorable to the business.

An amount set aside today for one year will earn interest. On a simple interest basis its future FV after one year will be equal to the original amount A_0 plus the interest I:

$$FV_1 = A_0 + I = A_0 (1+i) \tag{1}$$

where i is the annual interest rate.

FV can be expressed to reflect continuous compounding, which is appropriate to periods of high interest rates:

$$FV_1 = A_0 e^i \tag{2}$$

where e is the base of Naperian logarithms.

An amount set aside for a longer period t, in the annual interest and continuous compounding cases, respectively, will have a future value of:

$$FV_t = A_0 (1 + i)^t \tag{3}$$

or

$$FV_t = A_0 e^{it} \tag{4}$$

where t is time measured in years.

The present value of any future amount can be found from Eqs. (3) or (4) by dividing the time-dependent term. Thus, the net present value of the stream of future R&D expenditures can be discounted to the present time and summed, and so can the stream of future benefits, which makes possible a comparison of the two on a common time scale.

As this process is followed by most firms for capital expenditures, a threshold interest rate will normally be available reflecting the firm's analysis of its cost of money (Quirin, 1967). At this threshold rate, the net present value of the benefits from a research decision should be equal to or greater than the net present value of the costs of R&D plus all other associated start-up costs such as those for manufacturing and marketing.

A little reflection on the effect of discounting leads to two basic conclusions. First, at any effective interest rate, the present value of future benefits must exceed the present value of costs so that undiscounted benefits must far exceed costs. This is the fundamental source of a number of "rules of thumb" that exist in the folklore of most industrial research departments relating the minimum ratio of future net income or future sales required for approval of an R&D project.

Omega Scientific Laboratories, a subsidiary of a larger concern, was engaged in longer-range types of research. At one of its late-1960s business planning reviews, its research director told of using a ratio of 300 for future sales to research costs. As the company's return on sales was then 5% and its income tax rate was about 50% at the time, this was the equivalent of calling for a ratio of 30 times pre-tax income to research costs, or about 3 times pre-tax income to the total of research, development, manufacturing, and marketing start-up costs for a typical product in a company where the latter three costs were 9 times that of research.

This case highlights that research may only be the "tip of the iceberg" of costs to the company for following a given line of technological action. One reference places development expense at 20% of total evolution expenditures on an all-industry average (Booz-Allen, 1975, p. 10), which would imply all other expenditures such as manufacturing and marketing start-up are 4 times research and development costs. A second study places manufacturing development at 9 times R&D costs, and "retrofit of production" at 90 times R&D

expense (Block, 1979, p. 98). This latter factor presumably represents the extreme of a capital-intensive process industry. The factor of 9 used in the example was typical of a then vertically integrated full-line manufacturer. The factor of 4 in the first reference was stated as an all-industry average. The author's recent experience with minimally integrated (assembly and test only) electronics firms which have large research and development investments in computer software show factors for other costs less than 1 times R&D. To recapitulate the first conclusion, the future value of benefits must exceed the future value of all evolution costs, only part of which in research and development may be under the research manager's control.

The practice of discounting also suggests that the longer it takes from the start of R&D to the start of net income, the higher must be the ratio of benefits to costs. This is the primary reason for the relatively large fraction of short-term projects in the typical industrial research program. The effect of discounting is to make long-term projects profitable only if their perceived return is large.

As a preface to the next example, it is appropriate to define a specific financial measurement, *the internal rate of return*, which will be more fully developed and compared with other yardsticks in Chapter 5. The internal rate of return (IRR) is that interest rate which equates the net present value of benefits with that of costs. It assumes (by definition) that cash inflows are reinvested at the same rate of return. Most financial textbooks give a discussion of this assumption's implications which have a minimal impact on R&D investment (Van Horne, 1974).

Psi Radio Limited, a subsidiary of a multinational company, has a labor- and material-intensive electronic product line where, a few years ago, the sum of marketing and manufacturing start-up investment nearly equaled R&D costs. Its product development cycle was then typically three years with each year accounting for about 25, 50, and 25% of the total project cost, respectively. Its product sales life cycle of about five years gave each year, respectively, about 7, 27, 32, 27, and 7% of cumulative net income for the five years.

Psi Radio used the IRR yardstick for local project approval, based on the full five year cycle. The parent company, however, used only the ratio of three years net income to projects costs. One division manager produced the graph shown in Figure 2.1 as an aid in translation between these two methods of measurement.

Figure 2.1 shows the IRR calculated for delays from the start of R&D to the start of net income of from one to four years plotted against

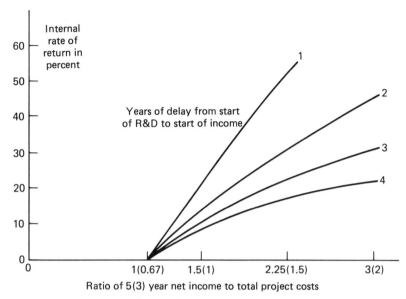

Figure 2.1. Internal rate of return versus project costs and delay

the ratio of net income to total project costs. At net income equal to 2.25 times costs, the effect of going from a one to four year delay is to drop the IRR from 54 to 16%. For a 20% IRR, a project delayed one year needs less than a 1.5 ratio of net income to R&D costs, whereas a project delayed four years needs a 2.6 ratio.

One result of looking at R&D projects with financial yardsticks measuring the time value of money is the shortened time horizons associated with recent high inflation and high interest rates. Also, the examples given above are from periods when tax rates were equal and unchanging on R&D expense and on benefits. With the adoption in the United States of the *Economic Recovery Act of 1981*, new tax incentives for R&D have made it necessary to look at similar assessments now on an after income tax basis precisely because these incentives have been set on an incremental basis.

MOST DECISIONS ARE MADE AT THE MARGIN

A basic principle of economics is that returns diminish as activity increases. On a macroeconomic basis, business activity tends toward the level that just keeps the marginal producer in business. Within a company, at the microeconomic level, not all activities are equally profitable. Thus, additional activities will be undertaken only if they are marginally profitable, that is, if the incremental benefits exceed the incremental costs.

The framers of the Economic Recovery Act of 1981 used this reasoning in setting the R&D incentive as an added tax credit of 25% only for increases in certain forms of research above the level of comparable effort in 1981. Thus, if a research decision had been made in 1981 with a benefit of 200 versus a cost of 100, its before and after tax benefit-to-cost ratio would have been 2. In 1982, at a 48% normal federal income tax rate, the after tax benefit would be 104, and the after tax cost only 27, for a benefit-to-cost ratio of 3.85 for a research project meeting the qualifications of the new act.

In the case of Psi Radio (Figure 2.1) a two year delay R&D project with a ratio of 1.5 of five year net income to project costs had only a 15% IRR at the time the chart was prepared. Had a tax credit of the 1981 form been available then, the same project (at Psi's then income tax rate) would have risen to an attractive IRR of 46%.

With this high multiplying factor on return, many previously marginal projects should have shown acceptable returns in 1982. Preliminary figures in mid-1982 showed the result, with 1982 R&D spending plans up 17% against an expected inflation rate of 6.5% for a real growth of over 10% (*Business Week*, July 5, 1982, p. 54). Thus, many firms made decisions at the margin in approving 1982 projects. Those that did not were either strapped for cash (equivalent to a higher required threshold rate), confused by the new tax law, or supercautious and content to add the credit (to the extent received because of inflation) to net income.

CASH FLOW PAYBACK

In contrast to the dual measures of return and time used in the previous sections, an often used measure is time alone. Cash flow payback is defined as the time required to return the original investment. In the case of a research decision this should properly reflect all start-up costs including R&D, manufacturing, and marketing.

The use of cash flow payback as a measure presumes that additional benefits will continue to occur after the payback period. This is the equivalent of the first conclusion in the first section, that the undiscounted value of benefits must exceed costs substantially. Its application in practice rests on two advantageous characteristics of the cash flow payback method.

The first of these is simplicity. One measure is easier to use than two. Any experienced R&D manager is aware that the degree of understanding of engineering economics by new engineers is a function not only of their own inclinations but also of the varying stress placed by engineering schools on this topic. The few scientists who have been exposed to an economics course have usually been taught only macroeconomics. But all engineers and scientists who have to work for a living have been personally exposed to the problems of cash inflow periodically and outflow continuously. Thus the simplicity of cash flow calculating make it a readily applicable tool in the research department.

One example of the efficacy of this technique occurred some 15 years ago in Omega Scientific Laboratories when enthusiasm for computer-aided design (CAD) techniques was just beginning. Naturally, the program for CAD ballooned to unmanageable proportions, with little thought for benefit-to-cost ratios. Cash flow payback was introduced as a self-disciplining procedure.

First, an approval threshold was established by noting that at that time net income after tax and R&D costs were about equal in the parent company. Since a 50% income tax rate was applicable, each unit of R&D cost was required to produce two units of pretax income. However, if engineers were to have been diverted to CAD, they would not have been producing net income in new products. Thus, a hurdle rate was established for CAD projects requiring that each unit of CAD cost should produce four units of pretax net income through cost reduction.

The engineers involved quickly accepted the challenge. When the program was resubmitted, it was for about three-quarters of the original amount. However, only half of the original projects were resubmitted, and the balance of the program was new projects selected from those that had been initially excluded as intellectually less interesting, but which on reflection looked very attractive from the point of view of benefits versus costs. The self-disciplining nature of cash flow payback was retained by the project leaders and applied to subsequent years' budget submissions without further pressure from R&D management.

The second advantageous characteristic of cash flow payback is that its reciprocal is a good proxy for internal rate of return (IRR) under certain circumstances which tend to be met in the case of research decisions. This can be seen from the following derivation. By definition, the net present value of a decision is expressed by the following equation:

$$NPV = -Q_0 + \frac{P_d}{(1 + i)^d} + \frac{P_{d+1}}{(1 + i)^{d+1}} \cdots + \frac{P_n}{(1 + i)^n} \quad (5)$$

where Q_0 = the initial outlay (or its present value if multiyear)
P_t = cash inflow in year t
i = interest rate
d = delay in years in beginning cash inflow
n = years to last cast inflow

But the IRR is that rate which makes the net present value zero. If it is assumed that cash inflows (P) are equal, the delay is one year and the initial outlay is recovered in N years, then Eq. (5) is transformed as follows:

$$NPV = 0 = -NP + P \sum_{1}^{n} (1 + IRR)^{-t} \quad (6)$$

or dividing by P and rearranging

$$N = \sum_{1}^{n} (1 + IRR)^{-t} \quad (7)$$

multiplying Eq. (7) by $(1 + IRR)$

$$N(1 + IRR) = 1 + \sum_{1}^{n-1} (1 + IRR)^{-t} \quad (8)$$

subtracting Eq. (7) from Eq. (8) and dividing by N

$$IRR = \frac{1}{N} \left(1 - \frac{1}{(1 + IRR)^n} \right) \quad (9)$$

It can thus be seen that if there is a long delay to the last cash inflows, which is possible with a good research decision, and assuming a high internal rate of return, payback in years is a good proxy for the reciprocal of the internal rate of return. Thus, a 4 year payback, where inflows last 10 years, represents a 21.3% rate of return, not far from the 25% reciprocal of payback.

While most modern financial textbooks disparage the use of pay-back in capital budgeting, its combination of simplicity and relative accuracy, given the long delay inherent in the R&D process, make it a technique worth considering by the research manager.

OPPORTUNITY COST

Implicit in the foregoing sections is the assumption that there is an alternative use for available money. Rather than giving funds to the research department, the general manager may consider investment in other functions offering better opportunities. It is important, therefore, that the research manager understand the concept of opportunity cost.

First, opportunity cost is not accounting cost. Both include cash outlays for labor; overhead, and materials. Accounting cost, however, treats past capital outlays as items to be recovered in current costs through depreciation and interest. Opportunity cost focuses on the potential alternative use of inputs, including plant in place. It is calculated from the revenue that could be obtained from the use of the input in a different manner, after subtracting the costs associated with the alternate use.

One example involves the former location of an old research laboratory (Laboratoire Central de Telecommunications) near the center of Paris (Deloraine, 1976, Figure 16). Not only had the building been fully depreciated, but the land was carried at historical cost in French francs, a currency that had undergone a great deal of inflation.

Thus, depreciation and interest costs were low from an accounting standpoint, and there was a strong tendency to consider this an advantage because it kept R&D costs low.

When viewed from the vantage point of opportunity cost, remaining in the old location was the wrong decision. The building had no real opportunity cost, but the current value of the land was very high because of its prime location. Thus, the opportunity cost of remaining at the present site was very high; economic costs could have been reduced by selling the old site and using less than half the proceeds to build a new modern laboratory in an attractive suburban location, while reinvesting the balance profitability elsewhere. Following an analysis based on opportunity cost, this is just what was done a few years ago.

The research manager operates on the opportunity side of the business, promising an economic return for today's expenditure. What must be guarded against is the operating focus of much of the rest of the business which treats costs in the accounting sense and tries to reduce them. But while defending the budget level against all attackers, one must be aware of the true opportunity costs of the department.

MARGINAL ANALYSIS

Marginal analysis studies the differences in costs and benefits due to management decisions that change business activity. In so doing, it assumes that fixed costs are sunk costs, that is, incapable of modification as activity levels fluctuate up and down. In terms of the calculus, it is the first derivative of benefits less that of costs. If the marginal profit is positive, there is an incentive for management to increase activity, even if fully distributed fixed costs are not recovered, up to the point where marginal costs equal marginal revenues.

In microeconomic theory, the application of marginal analysis to the entire operating entity means that conditions are curvilinear and nearly continuous so that the calculus may be used. In practice most individual decisions are more likely to be linear, and incremental analysis can be done algebraically or through linear programming. Although there is a large divergence in detail in the literature, the essential principal applies—if the analysis shows a positive marginal profit, activity should be increased up to the point where marginal profit is zero (Haynes and Henry, 1974, p. 16).

Most of the industrial world's export business is priced marginally, that is, all start-up costs, including research, development, manufacturing, and so on, are considered to be recovered only in the domestic market. Thus, added business from exporting the same products needs only to recover the incremental outlays in labors and materials, not full overheads, to be considered marginally profitable. The hazard is that another competitor will attack the privileged sanctuary of the first company's home market with its marginally priced product, at which point government intervention is usually called for to prevent "dumping."

An interesting example of a product that used to be traditionally marginally priced by European manufacturers was teleprinters, manufactured in electromechanical form through the 1970s by only a limited number of companies: Siemens and Lorenz (ITT) in West Germany, Creed (ITT) in the United Kingdom, and SAGEM in France. In the late 1960s, the entry model (keyboard send and receive) sold in the three domestic markets in the 1500–$2000 range, and in the rest of European countries in the 1000–$1200 range. With the advent of the Common Market (European Economic Community), a flourishing business began of buying teleprinters in a small country (such as Holland) and sending them back to their country of origin through used teleprinter dealers. Marginal pricing within Europe soon almost ceased.

As usual, there is a gap between theory and practice, for which three common reasons can be given. The first of these is financial rationing. The long-term financial planning of a corporation sets certain limits to the availability which is then parceled out to the business functions as objectives. The effective department manager often has more projects than the cash flow allocated to him or her can support, and is forced to ration at an activity level below the point of zero marginal profit. The importance of marginal or incremental analysis in this situation is that it makes possible a rank ordering of projects by marginal profit. Action can then take place on the breadwinners, and only those projects of low marginal contribution are curtailed. These points are covered in greater detail in Chapter 9.

A second reason for the gap between theory and practice is risk and uncertainty. Where there is a chance that the return will be lower than expected, or costs higher, a penalty may be added explicitly or implicitly to reject projects with small marginal profits. Chapter 6 sets out methods for handling risk and uncertainty.

The third reason for the practice–theory gap is that increases in activity can often only be done by price reductions. The many fares of airline companies are a classic example. The risk involved in this method of activity enhancement, however, is that there may be a shift in the formerly presumed high-margin customer's behavior to take advantage of the lower prices. In airline terminology, first-class passengers may choose economy fares and economy passengers may opt for supersaver fares, thus shifting downward the activity level of zero marginal profit.

GROSS CONTRIBUTION TO FIXED COSTS

Whereas marginal analysis may serve the needs of the individual function manager, the general manager of an operating unit needs techniques to put all of the functions together. Only if revenues exceed the total of fixed and variable costs at a particular activity level will net profits result. A typical break-even chart is shown in Figure 2.2.

The focus on gross contribution to fixed costs per unit of output is really a reflection on marginal profit. Because the slope of the revenue line below break-even is higher than the slope of the variable (marginal) cost line, a marginal profit ensues. Under these conditions below break-even, the general manager needs to seek higher-order

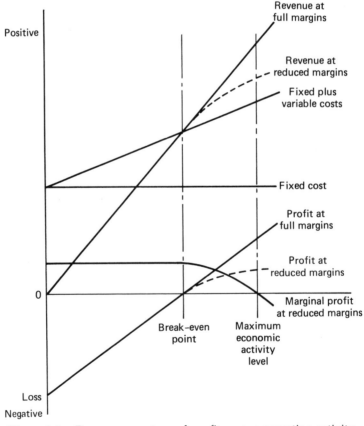

Figure 2.2. Revenues, costs, and profit versus operating activity

bookings to move above the break-even point, or to lower the fixed cost burden.

Above break-even in Figure 2.2, a second set of curves shows the effect of price discounting to achieve higher activity levels. The maximum economic activity level is the one where the slope of revenue at reduced margins is equal to the slope of variable cost, or where marginal profit is zero. At this level, either an increase or a decrease of activity will reduce total profit. At such a point, a close look at contribution would show that profits can only be increased by substituting full-margin orders for those of reduced margin.

Psi Radio Limited at one time was in a below break-even situation. Its consumer electronics division had ceased to contribute to profit even marginally and was disbanded. Even though fixed costs tied to consumer electronics were cut, the residue of fixed costs was a problem. The plant was too large for the remaining product lines, with over 1000 square feet of floor space per direct worker, and was laid out in a manner that virtually eliminated the possibility of subdividing it.

Based on the competitive situation, increasing activity domestically was difficult. Export was a possibility, but a studying of Psi's break-even chart showed that (below break-even) marginal pricing made no sense, as it pushed the revised break-even too far out. Only a limited number of products could be sold in world markets at domestic prices. These were made the subject of a successful export campaign that brought an additional contribution to fixed costs, but still not to break-even levels of activity.

The remaining factor in the chart was variable cost. The engineering department was set a task of designing lower cost replacement products which finally pulled the break-even point down below combined domestic and export sales volume. But lowering variable cost meant lowering direct labor hours, which made 11% of the workforce redundant.

Economies of Scale

The essence of economies of scale is the opportunity to lower variable unit cost by increasing fixed cost—in other words, the substitution of capital, research, or market development for labor and materials. The lowering of variable unit cost corresponds to lowering the slope of the variable cost line of Figure 2.2, and correspondingly raising the marginal profit line. This results in a larger gross contribution to fixed costs per unit of output, which raises the maximum economic activity level. The challenge to the research manager is to identify meaningful changes in product or process that will achieve the benefits of economies of scale. At the same time, the research manager is forewarned that the scale at which one aims should be that needed by the end user, not the maximum scale for which creative engineers can design.

One of the most spectacular instances of economies of scale was the initial decade of the International Communications Satellite Consortium (Snow, 1976). Costs per two-way telephone circuit (marginal costs) dropped from the first through the fifth satellites in steady progression ($46,300; $38,900; $10,800; $7800; $7200, respectively) as capacity climbed from 240 to 6250 circuits per satellite, and investment rose per satellite from $11 million to $45 million (fixed costs). Boosted by a booming international economy and tariffs lowered to reflect lowered costs, traffic rose to keep satellites about half full throughout the period.

DIMINISHING RETURNS AND OPTIMIZATION

One of the most pervasive empirical rules of human behavior is that which relates to the distribution of results from activity. Almost a century ago it was noted that personal wealth had a natural distribution in any economy. The few rich had a large portion of the existing wealth, while the many poor had a smaller share. Most research directors have noted a similar distribution in their own engineers and scientists—most of the worthwhile results come from a small fraction of the staff.

It should come as no surprise, therefore, that a similar distribution should occur in the distribution of potential research projects conceived by the R&D department, or by the marketing department. After a rank ordering of the projects, it is quickly noted that the per-project potential benefits drop steadily as the list of potential projects lengthens. This is known in economic terms as *diminishing returns,* and is shown graphically in Figure 2.3.

Several things are readily noted from this chart. On a smoothed basis, marginal benefits fall in the manner discussed so that cu-

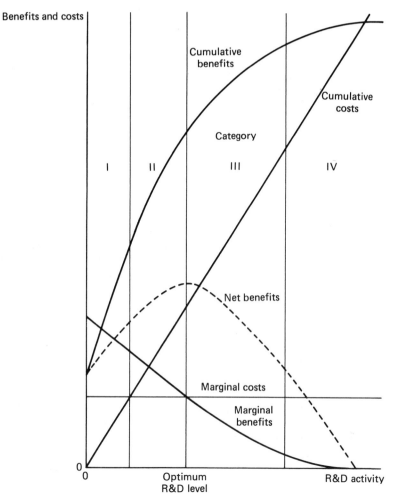

Figure 2.3. Benefits and costs versus R&D activity

mulative benefits nearly level off. Net benefits obtained by subtracting cumulative costs from cumulative benefits reach a peak where marginal benefits equal marginal costs, and then fall with higher activity levels. At this point there is an optimum level of R&D activity.

It is precisely because of his experience with setting objectives that the author attributes the nature of the curves in Figure 2.3 to an underlying diminishing returns in projects which are rank ordered from best to worst benefits. Only a handful of exceptions have been noted, despite spirited dissent from this approach (Rosenau, 1980).

In the late 1960s, the product line manager (PLM) of one of ITT Europe's telecommunications product lines had come to suspect that his department was not at an optimum level of R&D activity. The year is not important except to realize that issue was just beginning to be posed analytically, and answered only empirically (Sandretto, 1968, Chapter 2).

The specific product line was one of rapid technological change, with some 50% of sales in each country coming from products introduced in the previous three years. For this reason R&D expenses tended to the high side in some countries, to a high of 15% of sales. The PLM was convinced that this level was so high as to adversely affect profits but lacked objective answers as to how much should be spent.

A meeting was convened with senior technical and marketing staff from both ITT Europe and ITT headquarters at which was asked both how much should be spent on R&D and why. Ten ITT-affiliated companies in Europe and four elsewhere in the world manufactured a similar product liine. Not surprisingly for an independently managed group of companies (which until then had been only loosely coordinated), their ratios of R&D to sales were widely distributed from the high of 15 to a low of ½%. Even more interesting, however, was the spread of return on sales which bore the characteristic shape of the net benefits curve in Figure 2.3. Each company's strategy was individually critiqued and specific spend-less, spend-more, or hold-the-line objectives were generated. From this exercise, and comparable ones in other functional areas, came a master target used for several years: "seven and seven," that is, 7% R&D to sales and 7% return on sales (after tax).

Even where studies support this basic approach, some argument exists as to the location of the optimum point. One study argues that the maximum level of R&D activity that can be allowed is where net benefits have fallen back to their level with no R&D, because the firm is no worse off at that point (Gilman, 1978). Although this may be a plausible argument for a research manager to use to defend a higher budget, it does not stand the test of marginal economic analysis.

It will also be noted that some benefits exist when there is activity. Because of this, some short-term-oriented general managers may be inclined to underspend on research. An examination of published data shows a rather even distribution between low R&D levels and the levels of the various industry leaders, which may be presumed to be near optimum (*Business Week,* July 5, 1982, pp. 54–70). If we assume that few companies overspend the optimum R&D level, the part of the net benefit curve below this point can be approximated as a straight line to determine both the benefit at no R&D and the average marginal benefit. Such an analysis of four electronic-based industries was made in an earlier study (Ellis, 1980). While there was a rather broad spread of results and more not significant results than significant ones, this should not be considered surprising in the view of the fact that only one independent variable (R&D) was used for analysis when many other factors affect profit also. It should be cautioned that (mathematically) correlations is not causation, and the interpretation is based on the author's experience. The average growth in return on sales (after tax) was 0.41% in that study for each 1% increase in R&D-to-sales ratio. A spot check of the 1982 data for information processing: computers shows a growth in return of 0.35% for each percentage point increase in R&D-to-sales ratio. The exact values change from year to year by product category, but empirical support for a positive return on R&D spending is remarkably consistent in higher technology industries (Parasuraman & Zeren, 1983). It should be noted that this is the benefit resulting from past research, not current research. Since the ratio of R&D to sales changes slowly in most companies, this factor is approximately correct when comparing current return to current research.

Figure 2.3 has been divided into four categories: I, above average marginal benefit; II, between average and zero marginal benefit; III, negative marginal benefit, but net benefits above no R&D activity; and IV, activity with nearly no marginal benefits, only costs. The first category is clearly the mainstream of the research program and easy to defend to general management. Programs in this group ensure the future growth and profitability of the firm.

The other categories are less easy to defend. Although there is positive marginal profit in the second category, it is diminishing. It is hoped that this category will encompass products complementary to the first category or clearly productive specialties. The term *unproductive* is used here in an economic sense, not in a derogatory one. These are often potentially productive projects, yet because of the time value of money, may not show positive discounted present value, or may be in the category of "right, but too soon." Consider, as an example, an assertion by products marketing that it needs to meet the competition of the industry leader without discounted benefits exceeding costs. There may still be some advantage in including a number of the less productive programs in the budget, for reasons which will be substantiated in Chapter 5. Finally, projects in the fourth category can only be defined as unnecessary specialties. Those that are not mandated by government regulation should be rigorously pruned from the initial program submissions.

SUMMARY

Some underlying concepts of microeconomics have been reviewed from the vantage point of the research manager. Research decisions are made on costs and benefits at separated dates. Thus, all must be discounted to the present monetary units for comparison. The discounted benefits must be higher than research costs by an increasing amount as the start of net income is delayed. Cash flow payback is a simple single measure that has in its reciprocal an estimate of project return. Opportunity cost focuses on the alternative use of scarce resources. Marginal analysis looks at the relative net benefits of incremental decisions and accepts all activity with positive net benefits. Several reasons exist why there is a gap between theory and practice. The general manager must integrate the departmental functions and achieve an overall absorption of fixed costs in volume of activity. If demand permits, increasing fixed cost to reduce variable cost results in economies of scale. Eventually, however, diminishing returns are experienced, and marginal benefits fall below marginal costs. Some benefits exist at no R&D cost, and initially, the primary projects yield a high ratio of benefits to costs. The secondary projects are still productive, and the tertiary projects, while still yielding benefits, have negative marginal profits and represent above-optimum activity levels. The final category of low benefit projects need to be weeded out of the initial program suggestions.

EXERCISES

1. Assume the net benefit curve in Figure 2.3 is parabolic (Chapter 8 gives a rationale for such an assumption); that net benefits after tax benefits at no R&D are 3% on sales for Gamma Products' industry with an initial incremental improvement of 0.5% per

percentage increase in the R&D-to-sales ratio. Calculate for Gamma Products (Table 1.1) the R&D/sales ratio where net benefits are maximized and compare with actual R&D/sales ratios. Did Gamma follow an optimum strategy?

2. Considering the marginal analysis in Table 1.1, what is the IRR of the major R&D project? (If your hand calculator or accessible computer has no IRR program, solve graphically by calculating net present value at 10% increments and interpolating linearly). If the benefits of 1980 continue two years longer, what is then the IRR? If competitive conditions shorten the product's life so that 1981 benefits are 0.5, 1982's 0.1 and zero thereafter, how does this change the IRR?

3. Recalculate the IRRs of Exercise 2 with the assumption that the 25% incremental tax credit for R&D had been available in 1976, with a 50% normal tax rate.

4. Considering your answers to Exercises 2 and 3, how would you have changed Gamma's strategy from the one that it adopted if this were 1976? If this were 1982 and the incremental tax credit could be used?

REFERENCES

Block, Robert G., "Ten Commandments for New Product Development," *Industrial Research/Development*, March 1979, 98.

Booz-Allen & Hamilton, *Management of New Products*, New York, 1975.

Deloraine, E. Maurice, *When Telecom and ITT Were Young*, New York: Lehigh Books, 1976.

Ellis, Lynn W., "Optimum Research Spending Reexamined," *Research Management*, **23** (3): 22–24 (1980).

Gilman, John J., "Stock Price and Optimum Research Spending," *Research Management*, **21** (1): 24–26 (1978).

Haynes, W. Warren and William R. Henry, *Managerial Economics*, 3d ed., Dallas: Business Publications, 1974.

Joint Committee on Taxation of the U.S. Congress, Staff Paper, "Incentives for Research Experimentation," *General Explanation of the Economic Recovery Tax Act of 1981*, Washington, D.C.: Government Printing Office, 1981, 117–137.

Parasuraman, A., and Linda M. Zeren, "R&D's Relationship with Profits and Sales," *Research Management*, **26** (1): 25–28 (1980).

Quirin, C. David, *The Capital Expenditure Decision*, Homewood, IL: Irwin, 1967.

Rosenau, Milton D., "Problems With Optimizing Research Spending," *Research Management*, **23** (6): 7 (1980).

Sandretto, Peter C., *The Economic Management of Research and Engineering*, New York: Wiley, 1968.

Snow, Marcellus S., *International Satellite Communications*, New York: Praeger, 1976.

Van Horne, James C., *Financial Management and Policy*, Englewood Cliffs, NJ: Prentice-Hall, 1974.

3

THE STRUCTURE
OF RESEARCH AND
DEVELOPMENT COSTS

Research and development costs arise from cash outlays for wages, taxes, rents, and many other items. The sum of all of these outlays represents the research and development budget each year.

The work of a research department is task-oriented. The tasks have been defined as undirected research in areas of corporate interest, new products and processes for new markets, new products and processes for existing markets, and assistance to divisions with

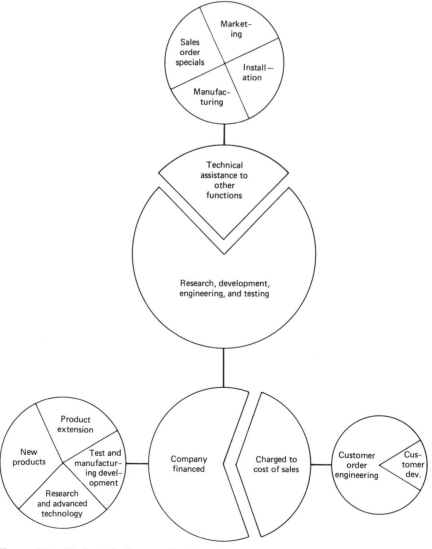

Figure 3.1. Technical effort evaluation chart. (From Sandretto, 1968. Copyright John Wiley & Sons, Inc.)

current problems (Gibson, 1981, pp. 159–160). Sandretto (1968, p. 3) categorizes these tasks as shown in Figure 3.1. Each of Sandretto's categories may be further subdivided into projects, studies, and so on as needed for measurement and control.

Although it is theoretically possible to calculate the details of the outlays for each task, it is impractical because of the drudgery involved. Thus, in the preparation of annual budgets, usually a rate per man-hour, man-day, man-month, or other unit of time, is calculated, with the active research worker treated as the accountant would a craftsman in a job shop. Costs other than wages are prorated on the active or direct worker's salary as overhead. The sum of direct hours over the year times the salary plus the overhead rate per hour must come to the same total monetary value as the sum of all cash outlays. Understanding the structure of R&D costs and the nature of required tasks is important ot adequate communication with management on projected R&D programs.

As mentioned in the example in Chapter 1, Alpha Electrical Industries Limited's switching manager felt secure in the mid-1960s in the choice of a semielectronic product (computer controlled, but still equipped with relays for switching) because AT&T's ESS had made the same choice. In fact, AT&T's decision reflected a serious failure of communication between the system group at Bell Labs to AT&T's top management as to the true nature of R&D and the production costs associated with this venture (Brooks, 1976, pp. 278–280).

Based on the system group's 1955 assessment of costs of the No. 1 ESS development, newly elected AT&T president Fredrick Kappel approved a development program of $45 million in 1956 and announced a 1959 completion date. With 20–20 hindsight vision, it should be noted that real-time software was such an unknown in 1955 that many other companies also missed estimates by large ratios. Even this source of error was not enough to explain the total development cost of $500 million and the delay in full implementation to the late 1960s. No. 1 ESS was a true innovation and required a change of behavior in the way it was made, tested, diagnosed, field serviced, and documented that went far beyond the system group's idea of its R&D task.

THE CONCEPT OF OVERHEAD

Overhead represents costs that are allocated indirectly to the time worked by active researchers.

Often when the comptroller is asked about the indirect costs of the technical department, he replies, "What do you mean by *indirect costs?* These costs represent overhead, and all of our technical activities constitute overhead" (Sandretto, 1968. p. 21).

Overhead is one of the aspects of financial cost accounts most confusing to the engineering manager. In this context, the previously mentioned analogy to a job shop is useful. The hours directly applied, or charged, to a job form the basis for accounting for time. In addition to the direct labor rate, however, the cost actually used must carry its fair share of the total cost of the shop or department. The difference between total and direct costs is overhead to the department head. To the extent, however, that R&D costs are not charged to customer contracts, the balance of indirect and direct R&D labor registers as an overhead charge to the general manager and comptroller when calculating the periodic profit and loss statements.

For the purposes of project selection, management, and contol accounting, despite the treatment used for financial reporting purposes, the department head's view of costs must prevail for research managers to do their jobs, as is the case with the manager of any job shop. In addition, research managers are responsible for keeping down their overhead rates (ratio of overhead to direct labor), so costs should be charged as directly as possible. This will place them in frequent conflict with the accounting professional, who will tend to prefer the convenience of allocation to the specific work of accumulation of actual costs. An example of a negotiated compromise (in a company we may call Delta Technology Inc., to mask its identity) is as follows, as adapted from the company's standard practice manual:

The confusion about classification of employees as direct or indirect arises from the use of these terms for two purposes. The first is the formal classification used for financial reporting. The second use is for calculation of department overhead rates. In some departments, most notably engineering, a person must be classified as an indirect employee for financial reporting purposes, but as a direct employee for the calculation of any meaningful department overhead rates. For example, a development engineer is an indirect employee, but should be counted as "direct" in the calculation of the development department overhead rate because he is spending the majority of his time on productive development work.

In order to put these concepts into application, the following decision rules should be used in the future for the classification of employees.

Financial Reporting

1. All employees in the following departments must be classified as *indirect*:

   Advanced Development

   Product Development

   Product Engineering

2. Employees in the following departments may be classified as either direct or indirect according to the guideline below:

   Project Engineering

   Project Management

   Project Commissioning

A *Direct*, if they charge more than 50% of their time to customer orders

B Otherwise, *indirect*

Budgeting (Overhead Rates)

1. Automatically consider *direct* if classified direct according to financial reporting

2. Classify as *direct* if indirect for financial reporting, but charge more that 50% of time to development projects

3. Classify all others *indirect*

RESEARCH, DEVELOPMENT, AND ENGINEERING COSTS

The engineering or R&D costs with which the technical manager must cope include direct salaries and wages, associated labor benefits (fringes), cost of time paid not worked, and spending, both discretionary and allocated. The ratio of the latter three to the first determines the lowest possible overhead rate (LPOR). Actual rates will be higher depending on policies for the allocation of supervision, support, and interface costs with other departments.

Direct Salaries and Wages

For the purpose of determining accurately what are R&D costs, all who work on specific research, development, or engineering projects should be considered as direct workers and charge time on time sheets. This group includes not only engineers and scientists, but also technicians, drafters, model makers, and so on. Recognizing that workers in these categories charge directly will require that estimates of their costs be included in project proposals.

A frequent practice is charging a "supported engineer" with technical support personnel included in the overhead rate. This approach suffers from two deficiencies: First, projects differ greatly in support requirements so that the costs do not get correctly allocated. Also, well-meaning attempts to cut the overhead rate often leave engineers undersupported and doing jobs that a lesser-paid individual could handle. Thus, direct charging of support personnel, at a lower appropriate labor and overhead rate for their level of salaries, often lead to lower overall R&D costs, as the correct allocation of people to tasks is facilitated. (Sandretto, 1968, pp. 21–23).

Associated Labor Benefits

The act of hiring an individual incurs costs for the firm in a direct relation to salaries and wages. Some of these are unavoidable such as the employer's share of social security, workman's compensation, unemployment insurance, and so forth. That is, they are unavoidable in the sense of being mandated by law, and research managers have only their own individual voices with which to petition legislators for relief.

Another portion of associated labor benefits reflects those fringes for which the firm has assumed responsibility either as a result of negotiations, to meet a social responsibility, or to compete with other employers in the region to facilitate the acquisition and/or the retention of staff. These benefits include various forms of insurance (medical, group life, accidental), pensions, and amenities (cafeteria, social affairs) to the extent that they are not fully covered by charges to employees. To research managers they are uncontrollable except to the extent that they (as members of management) can participate with other functional heads in the setting of their company's policies.

It is not unusual in the United States for associated labor benefits to run some 35% of wages and salaries. In some European countries, associated labor benefits run over 100% of salaries owing to a greater emphasis on social welfare, and mandated year-end and vacation bonuses, and the like. The average firm is caught between those companies in its area with more market power who press for continued betterment of fringes, and smaller, newer entrepreneurial firms who can pay higher wages simply because they have as yet to become saddled with an aging labor force who value the security that is associated with such fringe benefits.

Time Paid Not Worked

A different, but costly, form of fringe benefit is time paid for in wages and salaries but not worked by the employee. This includes vacations, paid public holidays, sick days, and discretional holidays (such as the bridging of public holidays into four- or more day weekends).

Since only that time actually on the job can rationally be charged by the hour or day, the cost of time paid not worked becomes another overhead rate. If we consider that an individual is paid for 52 five-day weeks per year, or 260 days, this rate may be calculated for a typical example:

Vacation	15 days
Paid public holidays	6 days
Sick days	3 days
Discretionary days	2 days
Total	26 days

Thus, of 260 days, 234 are worked, 26 are not worked, which means an 11.1% additional overhead rate for the cost of time paid not worked.

Spending

Money must be spent beyond salaries and wages to support a technical activity. Some of this is allocated from the central expenses of the firm, and some is discretionary under the research manager's control.

First, floor space is occupied by the manager's department. The costs of occupancy include depreciation of the building, heating and cooling, maintenance, real estate taxes, and so forth. Normally, the sum of all these costs is apportioned by accounting on a "per square foot" basis.

A second usually apportioned charge is for depreciation of equipment used specifically by the engineering department. Other allocated charges may be for shares of other common services, such as the telephone system in the facility.

Discretionary spending relates to the range of items more directly under the research manager's control, such as:

Experimental materials
Recruiting and relocation expenses
Travel and conference expenses
Publications and instructional material
Computer operating costs and services
Temporary help and consultants
Small tools
Sales taxes on new equipment purchases to the extent that the purchases are controllable

If any of these (particularly materials and travel) are heavy, or unequally applied to the tasks of the department, it may make sense to cost them directly and to remove them from the overhead rate.

Lowest Possible Overhead Rate

In a department where everyone is directly charged to a job for time spent working, the lowest possible overhead rate (LPOR) would be the sum of discretionary and allocated spending plus cost of time paid not worked, plus the cost of associated labor benefits, all divided by the cost of direct labor hours (or days) worked. Given the examples used previously, this could be in the range of 75% in a typical department. It is often useful to calculate the LPOR to compare it with actual department rates, which reflect in addition the costs of supervision, support, and interfaces.

SUPERVISION AND SUPPORT COSTS

All personnel time unapplied to specific jobs affects the overhead rate in two ways. First, there is the cost of the unapplied time which affects the numerator of the rate calculation. And second, the subtraction from time applied lowers the divisor of the calculation.

Unapplied time, however, is inevitable. The manager's task is to keep it to a minimum. Consider first the manager's own time. Part of each week must be spent with the general manager, interfacing with other department managers, interviewing for new positions, preparing budgets and reports, and conducting many other tasks that are by their nature not assignable to a development project.

To a lesser extent, first-level supervisors have a similar inevitable need for unapplied time for many of the same reasons and tasks. They do, however, work much of their time on specific projects, so considering them as direct workers with a large unapplied time allowance is appropriate.

Clerical and secretrial support generally goes for so many diverse tasks not project related that it cannot be directly charged. Also, even direct workers need to be trained, attend conferences, and so on. An example of a 50 person research department showing the effect of unapplied time is shown in Table 3.1.

The sum of time paid not worked, plus unapplied time is now 30% of applied time. The shrinkage of applied time also raises the cost per direct hour (or day) for associated labor benefits and for spending. Thus, the lowest realizable overhead rate (LROR) is approximately 100%, rather than the 75% LPOR calculated earlier.

Many years of experience have shown that the LROR as defined in this section is the level for which a research manager should strive. To achieve it requires managing the external interface costs considered in subsequent sections.

Table 3.1. Departmental Allocation of Time at Delta Technology

No.	Title	Days paid	Paid not worked	Unapplied days	Applied days
1	Manager	260	26	234	—
2	Secretarial/ clerical	520	52	468	—
5	Supervisors	1,300	130	585	585
42	Staff	10,920	1,092	420	9,408
	Totals	13,000	1,300	1,707	9,993
	Percent Applied		13.0%	17.1%	

Source. Adapted by the author from proprietary data.

ASSISTANCE COSTS

The costs of assisting the peer departments of marketing, manufacturing, and installation or field service are often considerable. Depending on how organizational responsibilities are divided, they may amount to some 30% of total departmental time in a typical R&D organization.

Often, the financial manager has the philosophy that "it's all overhead anyway" and bans cross-charging. In a high-technology business, this often unfairly burdens the technical overhead rate since requests for help from the engineers usually exceed by far the assistance R&D needs from other departments. Worse still, the lack of cross-charging gives no accountability to the requesting department. Thus, calling for an engineer to come down to manufacturing or out to see a customer becomes an addictive habit for the requesting department. A policy of charging the requesting department keeps everyone honest, and the level of service desired can be negotiated in advance as part of the budgetary process.

The impact of various treatments of assistance costs can be seen in the examples of three companies. Delta, shown in Table 3.1, is a no-cross-charging company. Yet, for reasons discussed later, its overhead rate is only modestly above the LPOR.

Epsilon S.A. operates in a Latin country where social charges are high, and for cultural reasons, no engineer will accept an assignment to any department other than engineering. It also is a no-cross-charging company with excessive overhead.

Zeta Electronics Limited (in a third country) is a custom builder of systems with full cross-charging between departments.

Assistance to Marketing

Assistance to marketing takes a number of forms. First is detailed design or engineering on special orders. In addition, the marketing function may require assistance on the most complex proposals, assistance in customer presentations, support at trade shows or conferences, or help in technical negotiations. These assistance costs segregate naturally into two groups: those associated with an order that has been received and those that do not.

In the negotiations for a specific order, it is usually possible to estimate the costs of special engineering work. These costs should be priced into the contract, and recovered as job costs in cost of sales once the order is received and the "sales order special" R&D work commences. This procedure not only places the costs where they belong, but also gives an accountability to the work and a means of measuring when the proportion of special work is in excess of the budgeted ratio to sales.

Delta and Zeta both handle specials by pricing them into the contract, even though specials are a low fraction of Delta's business and almost all of Zeta's work. Epsilon treats specials as overhead and thus has no control over them.

A special and analogous case is the provision to Marketing of equipment for demonstration and training. Since the equipment will eventually be placed in a capital account in that department, the work to be done should be estimated and charged directly to the capital account or to an intermediate work order it if facilitates cost accounting procedures.

The balance of assistance to marketing costs should be charged to an account number that is transferred to that department. The marketing manager is thus given the choice of paying and budgeting for this service, or equipping the marketing department to handle the majority of customer technical servicing. While the engineering manager may consequently face a periodic drain of manpower shifted to marketing, this loss is usually found preferable to a high level of unscheduled demands for assistance by key people.

Zeta is the only one of the three companies that charges Marketing for assistance. Since its business is customizing, it is logical that the engineers who write its proposals be the ones responsible for executing successful orders. Cross-charging puts the costs where they should appear for managerial control.

Delta's Marketing Department has its own technically competent support group, which needs little assistance from the R&D Department. With the consequent unapplied time low, R&D costs are only lightly penalized by assistance to Marketing.

Because all engineers at Epsilon are in R&D, all proposal writing is done in the Engineering Department and absorbed into R&D overheads. This adds about 50% to the engineering overhead rate, and makes marketing expenses appear unrealistically low.

Assistance to Manufacturing

Assistance costs to manufacturing fall naturally into those associated with capital equipment, those associated with start-up, and continuing engineering assistance. The extent of such assistance is a function of the rate of new product or process introduction and the technological competence of manufacturing (industrial) engineering.

Costs associated with capital equipment are inherently estimatable and should form part of the project proposal. Special manufacturing development should be treated in the research department as direct costs on a project regardless of the final accounting approach as to expensing or capitalizing of the costs.

Start-up costs are a natural consequence of new product or process introduction. As such, they can also be estimated in advance for a specific period of time into the transfer phase of technology. As such, they should be considered direct costs to the project. Some negotiations with the manufacturing manager will be necessary to define what time period needs to be covered in the development project.

Costs of assisting manufacturing after the agreed start-up period for any new product or process should be cross-charged to that department. Facing charges for such routine assistance, the manufacturing manager may rather staff his own department to handle the majority of such regularly occurring needs. Again, the research manager may face a drain of skilled talent, but this is often more effective than random and urgent requests for an engineer down on the factory floor for troubleshooting.

Neither Delta's engineering manager nor its manufacturing manager are happy with the no-cross-charging rule in that company. The engineering manager is irritated at the level of requests for assistance affecting unapplied time. The manufacturing manager equally has to absorb into unapplied time the costs of making mechanical parts for engineering models, which keeps the engineering manager's spending level below a true value. These offsetting actions probably do not have a material impact on Delta's engineering overhead rate.

Epsilon, however, finds its level of untransferred assistance to manufacturing adds another 20% to its overhead rate.

At Zeta, the engineering and manufacturing managers have negotiated a standard cost for assistance to manufacturing at 2½% of factory cost (about 1½% of sales or 12% of the RD&E budget). Overages and underages are treated as variances of engineering costs, not manufacturing costs.

All that has been said with regard to manufacturing applies equally to the rapidly growing field of automatic testing. Whether it is organizationally located in the manufacturing or quality control department, automatic testing is an implementation function and should be subject to the same rules of charging assistance costs.

Assistance to Installation and Service

Installation is equally an implementation function, and follows rules analogous to manufacturing. Assistance on capital projects should be so charged. Start-up costs on the first new installation should be forecast in the engineering project and not be passed along in cross charges. Subsequent contracts, however, should include any necessary R&D department assistance in job costs. In this manner, the installation manager can choose to add staff with the necesary skills or to budget for a preestimated level of engineering assistance.

Assistance to field service should also follow similar rules. It is important to note, however, that installation and field service skill levels are usually well below that of the technical department, and organizing for support for an extended period may well be an assignment on the technical manager's agenda. To protect the highly skilled people needed for research and development from these recurring demands, the creation of a buffer support department should be considered. This is especially important at times of major technical discontinuities such as when a mechanical product company starts to go electronic for the first time.

Delta does not cross-charge assistance to field service, but treats installation commitments as sales order specials. Zeta treats both as contract engineering and fully charges the cost of sales. Both keep this work under a single supervisor, creating in effect a buffer support department.

At Epsilon, a single supervisor also controls this activity, but it again is charged overhead, which adds some 40% to the engineering overhead rate.

GENERAL MANAGEMENT INTERFACES

The costs of interfacing with the general manager, and the remaining functional managers in such departments as finance and personnel, need to be considered for completeness. They are, however, almost impossible to budget, track, and control in the manner proposed above for assistance to marketing, manufacturing, installation and service. Since they largely involve the manager/supervisor level, they should be considered part of supervision costs in overhead.

THE TECHNOLOGICAL COMMUNITY

One final interface cost is that of interfacing with the technological community at large. Some of this cost will apply naturally to supervision, some to publications, and some to time for attending conferences.

In almost any organization, there are individuals who naturally and because of self motivation follow the changes occurring in the technological community to a greater extent than their average peers. Their activity is of great value to a research and development department, and they are frequently consulted by others for advice. It is in the interest of the research manager to support such "gate keepers" and budget for their unapplied time at a higher than average rate as the most cost-effective manner of keeping the technical workforce in touch with the fast-changing technical world.

The extent of all these different practices makes the overhead rates in the R&D departments of the three companies very different. Delta's engineering overhead is 137% (this will be derived later). Zeta's rate is only slightly higher at 152%, principally because of higher social charges than Delta.

At Epsilon, however, the rate is 450% from a combination of all the above mentioned effects. Rates of up to 600% are not uncommon in some European countries. Quantitative project justification is difficult under such conditions where charges to projects do not reflect true development costs.

On the other hand, in some contracts with the U.S. Defense Department, many of the costs treated in this chapter from a manufacturer's viewpoint are allowed as direct costs at standard rates. Such allowances as 2½ days vacation and 1 day sick leave per month when treated as applied time increases the denominator and lower the numerator in rate calculations.

DRAFTING THE BUDGET

The first step in drafting a departmental budget is to summarize all outlays. Usually the financial manager or comptroller will specify in detail by account number what format is to be used, and will also generate formulas for fringes that may be different for hourly, weekly, and monthly paid employees. Central allocations will be specified for floor space, utilities, depreciation, and so forth.

The department manager is responsible for the level of spending and for the number of people employed and their levels of responsibility. The actual budget level is negotiated with general management, as covered in Chapter 8.

As an example, a step-by-step budget calculation is shown in Table 3.2.

The wages and salaries for the people shown earlier in Table 3.1 are priced out by labor grade. It will be noted that a large gap exists between the supervision/senior engineer level and more junior staff salaries. Delta had once calculated a single labor rate for all staff employees. This led to supervisors recruiting too many senior engineers because better results were obtained for no higher charges

Table 3.2.   1980 R&D Department Budget at Delta Technology by Type of Outlay

Concept	Unit Cost ($)	Total Cost ($)
Wages and salaries		
Manager	55,000	55,000
Secretarial/Clerical (2)	15,000	30,000
Supervisors (5)	40,000	200,000
Sr. engineers (10)	33,000	330,000
Jr. engineers (15)	24,000	360,000
Technicians (9)	21,000	189,000
Drafters (8)	18,000	144,000
	Subtotal	1,308,000
Fringes (35%)		457,800
	Subtotal	1,765,800
Spending for travel, materials, etc.		330,000
Central allocations for floorspace, depreciation		202,000
	Total budget	2,297,800

Source.   Adapted by the author from proprietary data.

to the supervisor's project. To encourage the use of junior engineers and keep total engineering costs in line, a lower rate was set up grouping them with technicians and drafters, as will be seen in subsequent computations.

Fringes were calculated based on the comptroller's formulas, and central allocations were also supplied by the accounting department.

Spending in Delta's budget is somewhat out of line for a normal R&D operation. At the time, several projects were nearly completed. There were large materials expenses for models for test and for handover to manufacture, and there were large instruction book expenses. Accounting considered this an anomaly and demurred from shifting these items from R&D overheads for one year only.

Another large item was computer operation and service costs, which were also heavy owing to the fact that the software part of the project's cycle was handled in 1980. The choice of rate categories meant that hardware engineer overheads were carrying some computer costs beign incurred by software engineers, while software

Table 3.3. Calculation of 1980 Daily Rates at Delta Technology

Concept	Total salaries ($)	Applied days	Salaries applied ($)
Category A			
Supervisors	200,000	585	90,000
Sr. engineers	330,000	2,240	284,308
Subtotals		2,825	374,308
Category B			
Jr. engineers	360,000	3,360	310,154
Technicians	189,000	2,016	162,831
Drafters	144,000	1,792	124,062
Subtotals		7,168	597,047
Total			971,355

$$\text{Overhead rate} = 100 \times \frac{2,297,800 - 971,355}{971,355} = 136.56\%$$

$$\text{Category A rate} = \frac{374,308 \times 2.3656}{2825} = \$313.43/\text{day}$$

$$\text{Category B rate} = \frac{597,047 \times 2.3656}{7168} = \$197.03/\text{day}$$

Source.   Calculations from Tables 3.1 and 3.2.

engineer overheads were carrying some materials costs being in-curred by hardware engineers. Accounting considered the distortion minimal, and so another compromise was made in not costing hard-ware and software engineering separately in the interest of simplicity.

The actual calculation of rates is shown in Table 3.3. The salaries are as shown in Table 3.2 and applied days as shown in Table 3.1. Salaries applied is the fraction of total salaries proportional to the ratio of applied-to-total days. For supervisors

$$\$200,000 \times \frac{585}{1300} = \$90,000$$

The overhead rate is the total of all unapplied costs, spending, and allocations divided by applied salaries. Another way of express-ing this is as follows:

$$\text{Overhead rate} = 100 \times \frac{\text{budget minus applied salaries}}{\text{applied salaries}}$$

The actual rate of 136.56% is higher than the LPOR because of the higher spending mentioned above and because of the reasonably generous unapplied time allowances shown in Table 3.1. Part of the latter was because of a no-cross-charging between departments rule at Delta.

The calculation of the two rates for supervisors and senior engi-neers (Category A) and other staff (Category B) is then just as follows:

$$\text{Daily rate} = \frac{\text{salaries applied}}{\text{applied days}} \times \frac{100 \text{ plus overhead rate}}{100}$$

The more than 50% differential of A over B was a strong incentive to hire Category B people and train them in the department.

Finally, these hourly rates were assigned to projects as shown in Table 3.4. The development projects shown in Table 3.4 were ap-proved. Internally to the R&D Department, more project numbers were used for control to separate hardware and software develop-ment tasks, to break larger tasks into subtasks of several hundred man-days each, and to separately cost each sales order special.

One caution is in order regarding the low assistance level of Table 3.4. Delta had a large sales support group in marketing that kept

*Table 3.4.   1980 R&D Department Budget at Delta Technology
by Tasks*

| Concept | Days by category | | Costs equal |
	A	B	days times rates
Development projects			
Microprocessor converter	850	2,150	690,030
Micaconta driver	426	840	299,026
Heavy ion meter	377	805	276,772
Confabulator	327	723	244,944
Monitor system	822	2,300	710,808
Assistances			
Sales order specials	23	350	76,170
Assistance to other departments	In unapplied time		
Rounding error			50
Totals	2,825	7,168	2,297,800

Source.   Derived from Tables 3.1 to 3.3.

assistance to marketing low compared with many other companies and divisions, and assistance to Manufacturing was low at that time in Delta. For reasons given earlier in this chapter, the author does not support burying assistance to other departments in unapplied time as was done at Delta Technology.

SUMMARY AND CONCLUSION

The need has been outlined for managing internal and external interface technical costs on a "job shop" basis, at least for the purposes of project selection, measurement, and control. Financial accounting may, however, dictate final disposition of such project costs in the accounts as an overhead expense.

Technical department overheads are all costs associated with running the department other than the direct costs of wages and salaries for the time individuals work on projects. These include associated labor benefits (fringes), time individuals are paid that they do not work on projects, and both allocated and controllable spending. The lowest possible overhead rate is that rate which would occur if all possible time were charged to projects.

The realized overhead rate, however, has to reflect the costs of supervision, support, and interfaces. Supervision and support need to be minimized as overheads by having all individuals charge directly to projects whenever possible. Interface overhead costs need to be minimized by having the marketing and implementation costs cross-charged to the respective departments, who will then have the option to do more with their own people instead of obtaining "free" assistance from the technical staff. Other interfaces to general management, other functions, and the outside technical community can only realistically be handled by overhead allowances.

The research manager's task is to plan, budget, organize, measure, and control overhead costs as closely as possible to the lowest realizable overhead rate.

EXERCISES

1. For 1980, Delta's extraordinary spending items were divided between hardward and software engineers. In 1981, software engineering purchased a new computer, raising its spending by $112,000. The completion of product releases dropped hardware engineering's spending by $39,000. Accounting still refused to separate hardware and software rates. Software engineering comprised two sections heads, four senior engineers, and six junior engineers. Calculate software and hardware rates as if departments were separate (assume no inflation). Should the R&D manager have fought accounting's ruling?

2. You are asked to come in with a revised 1981 budget at 5% below 1980 (assume no inflation). Devise a strategy for the R&D department deciding how much to cut of A people, B people, spending, and so forth, and prepare the corresponding budget revision.

REFERENCES

Brooks, Frederick P., *The Mythical Man Month—Essays in Software Engineering*, Reading, MA: Addison-Wesley, 1975.

Brooks, John, *Telephone—The First Hundred Years*, New York: Harper & Row, 1976.

Dodson, Edward N., "Technological Change and Cost Analysis of High Technology Systems," *IEEE Transactions on Engineering Management*, **EM-24** (2): 38–45 (1977).

Gibson, John E., *Managing Research and Development*, New York: Wiley, 1981.

Gray, Irwin, *The Engineer in Transition to Management*, New York: IEEE Press, 1979. *See* particularly Chapter 4, "Responsibility for the Bottom Line."

Haynes, W. Warren, and William R. Henry, *Managerial Economics*, Dallas: Business Publications, 1974. *See* particularly Part Three, "Production and Cost."

Salmonson, R.F., Roger H. Hermanson, and James Don Edwards, *A Survey of Basic Accounting*, Homewood, IL: Irwin, 1981. *See* particularly Chapter 13, "Accounting in Manufacturing Companies."

Sandretto, Peter C., *The Economic Management of Research and Engineering*, New York: Wiley, 1968.

4

THE TIME DIMENSION OF RESEARCH AND DEVELOPMENT

Research and development has as its final objective a new or extended product, service, or process. Just as important as looking at all tasks of R&D within a given budget year (the subject of the previous chapter) is looking at all tasks within a time dimension broad enough to encompass the ultimate objective of R&D. This objective will usually be referred to in this chapter as a product since new products are the dominant focus of most R&D departments.

Every product that is launched has its own multiphase cycle from introduction to ultimate withdrawal from the market. The length of this cycle has several implications for the nature of the R&D process. First, there is the profitable part of the life cycle, the payback for the R&D effort—the return on R&D investment that determines the overall profitability of the firm. Second, the cycle acts as a clock that regulates new product initiation because to sustain growth a replacement or extended product must be available before the first product commences its decline. Product management, which is generally considered to be a marketing function, thus becomes one of the governing forces of a research and development department, specifying what, when, and how much.

The period before product introduction is when most research and development activities take place. The state of the art in advanced technology and applied research is a second governing force since too little innovation may lead to uncompetitive products and too much may lead to missing the appropriate market window for the product. The tradeoff between advanced technology and applied research on the one hand, and product and process development on the other is another of the decisions faced by the R&D manager that is affected by the broad time dimension.

The whole time cycle of R&D from early exploration and pioneering through commercialization has its phases. At each phase, costs mount on a cumulative basis. Also at each phase there is a mortality of new product ideas, as some are found to be not technically feasible, and some of those technically possible are found not to be commercially feasible.

When the R&D time cycle and product life cycle are considered together, there is a multiyear time dimension to each whole project. Every successful project results from an extended term contract between R&D and marketing to execute their respective portions of a project. A company's new product program can be managed effectively if there is organization and control over the entire project life, not just within the R&D and marketing departments separately.

PRODUCT LIFE CYCLES

The product life cycle has different forms in the perception of respected authors (Levitt, 1965; Booz-Allen & Hamilton, 1975). It also has different forms in the perception of managers in many industries. For example, to a toy manufacturer, often a product life cycle extends from introduction in March of a given year to decline at the end of the Christmas buying season of the same year. On the other hand, in some tradition-bound industrial product areas, products, once in the catalog, are there for decades.

There is a need to distinguish between innovation and invention. Innovation is the first commercial adoption of a product, and therefore is the start of the product life cycle. Invention is the first conceptualization of the product, and thus occurs at or before the beginning of the R&D life cycle, and often many years before innovation. Innovation may be continuous with new models performing the same function. It may also be dynamically continuous with jumps in technology but still the same user function (e.g., type basket to type ball to daisy wheel typewriters). Innovation may also

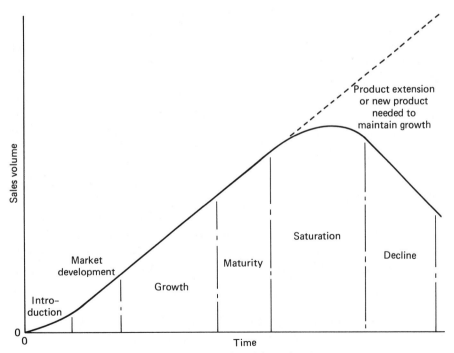

Figure 4.1. Product life cycle.

be discontinuous, at which point it often changes peoples' lives (e.g., radio to television).

For an innovation to be adopted, there must be not only a prospective return on investment to the manufacturer, but also a user's perception of relative advantage. This advantage may take such forms as compatibility, complexity, and divisability, or may be a matter of a lower price or lower operating costs to the end user. The communicability of this relative advantage may affect the speed of adoption of an innovation, and thus the length of the product life cycle.

A composite of several views of the product life cycle is shown in its phases in Figure 4.1. The separate phases of introduction, market development, growth, maturity, saturation, and decline are discussed in detail below. What comes after decline tends to be industry dependant, with a range from total withdrawal from the market (e.g., consumer products) to selective product pruning to virtually indefinite life (e.g., nuts, bolts, and screws).

Introduction Phase

The introduction phase is the initial step in bringing a new product to market. In some industries it is indistinguishable from the market development phase (e.g., consumer products). In industrial products, however, the two phases are often separate with the introductory phase using catchwords "Sample and see" or "Buy one and try one." The separate introduction phase is caused by user conservatism ("Someone is going to make a mistake, but it's not going to be me") and by the realities of product liability legislation and/or court decisions which make product qualification testing an obligation for manufacturer and user alike.

For the R&D manager, this phase in the product life cycle often overlaps the final phases of the R&D life cycle covered in detail later in this chapter. This is because sometimes results obtained from the later phases of testing on the consumers' premises (beta tests) indicate a need for further development. Because the product has moved to selected customers for their evaluation and approval (known as *qualification*), the introduction phase of the product life cycle has commenced.

Once a product has passed qualification tests at the manufacturer and by the introductory group of customers, the product may be considered to be introduced from the product manager's point of view. Once the necessary and/or desired and agreed changes have been identified and successfully manufactured, the product development cycle is considered complete by the R&D manager.

Market Development Phase

Once the product is clear of qualification testing, the market development phase begins in earnest. The essential objective of this phase is to stimulate demand for the product and set it on a growth mode. Depending on the product and the nature of its markets, this phase may include advertising, trade shows, demonstrations, responding to inquiries, or other means of diffusing knowledge about the product to an increasingly wider variety of customers. The length of this phase depends on the product's differentiation from others on the market and the customers' perception of the product's value to themselves. The history of the pharmaceutical industry, for example, is full of new wonder drugs with rapid market development because of high differentiation and real user needs in the fight against disease.

To the R&D manager, the market development phase for a specific product is a period of relative inactivity. The basic R&D cycle is complete, and it usually is too early to have enough market feedback to discuss intelligently potential product enhancements. In a multiproduct company the manager's resources may now be focused on other products earlier in their R&D life cycle. If the product development effort has been a large one, cutbacks may be made in the R&D program to provide funds for market development efforts—ideally, marketing will take some of the surplus in engineers to man market support activities.

Growth Phase

If the product is a technical but not a commercial success, its commercial life may end with the market development phase. A product that is to become commercially successful, however, will usually take off by itself some time after the demand-creating phase has started. This is the growth phase characterized by rapid increases in order intake. It is also the phase characterized by the beginning of competitor reaction.

The marketing emphasis shifts in this phase from having to create new customers, as in the previous phase, to convincing customers that this is the right product and should be ordered instead of competitors' products. In consumer goods this is often called the "battle for shelf space." New channels of distribution are opened, and these outlets begin to feed back newly desired differentiated features. The increased volumes of product sales and manufacturing's maturing learning curve tend to make the growth phase the one of highest profit margins. The impression of high profitability in turn spurs the competition to introduce further new products or commence price competition as a means of market share enhancement.

It is at the end of the growth phase that the need becomes obvious for reintroduction of the R&D department into the product life cycle. The differentiated features that will sell become known; the needs of newly opened distribution channels become visible; and the prospective cost levels to be profitable later in the product life cycle call for design cost reduction and/or new process development. Project selection activities begin looking toward product extensions or new products to maintain business growth.

Maturity and Saturation Phases

Either the reaction of competitors or market saturation can bring maturity to a product. Distribution channels become fully stocked, and the rate of new order input at the manufacturer level falls in an accelerating manner. Marketing begins to focus more on the end customer as a means of stimulating ultimate demand, and less on the distribution channels. Incentive programs begin ("extra green stamps").

The length of the maturity and saturation phases is very industry sensitive. In consumer goods and in women's fashions, it is very short. In many industrial goods the cycle is very long, with those companies having cost leadership slowly dominating what ultimately become commodity market places.

Maturity may be looked at as the end of growth, and saturation as no growth, or growth limited only to the population growth rate. The length of each of these phases is important to the R&D manager as a measure for timing the start of the R&D life cycle and the needed rate of progress.

Decline Phase

A market in decline is characterized by production overcapacity, leading to price cutting until weaker manufacturers fall one by one to the wayside. Process improvements leading to lower costs tend to dominate the requests of support from the R&D department. Mergers, acquisitions, and takeovers of product lines from other manufacturers all have an impact on the R&D managers' activity in those companies with a potential to survive. Product pruning is used to reduce the variety of surviving products and, it is hoped, increase the latters' production volumes.

Process and Service Life Cycles

Process and service life cycles have characteristics similar to product life cycles. Service life cycles are the most similar, yet few service activities are R&D intensive so that the R&D/product life cycle relationship mentioned above may not be analogous.

Chi Data Services Bureau was a service industry with a strong software R&D department. Its new services were focused on user industry segments. Thus, its R&D programs included credit checking data base administration for credit bureaus, electronic funds transfers packages for banking, and multiple airline reservation system access packages for travel agents. Each of these went through R&D and service life cycles, as did products, and required similar considerations for service life extensions.

Process life cycles may be similar to product life cycles, where the product and its process are inextricably intertwined. They may, however, be quite separate, where process development activities are delayed in time to the product extension phase. A frequent example is chemical and pharmaceutical products whose initial production is by a batch process. As the growth phase gets underway, volumes finally become high enough to support a continuous process, whose development is undertaken to lower production costs during maturity and saturation.

Product Extension Planning

Product managers in marketing departments can often be carried away by the glamour of new products. Such subjective instincts, however, need to be measured objectively against the business attractiveness of product extensions. Product extension planning early in the product life cycle can often be a very productive activity of product and R&D management. This is because the extension of product life may permit the reuse of skills attained in the R&D department, facilities established in the manufacturing departments, and customer contacts established in the sales department, at lower marginal costs than new product launches.

An example is the evolution of nylon by DuPont (Levitt, 1965). Launched during wartime, nylon had its initial uses in military applications (parachute fabric and cords, rope), but was originally developed for the circularly knit hosiery market. This latter market was extended several times with tinted, patterned, and textured hosiery, and with pantyhose.

Further extensions, with process development, came with broad-woven fabrics and warpknit fabrics for women's fashions. Then came a series of yarn process developments yielding tire cords, textured yarns for sweaters and socks, and yarns for carpets. These all kept nylon on a twenty year growth curve, allowing it to avoid saturation as its initial uses matured.

ADVANCED TECHNOLOGY AND APPLIED RESEARCH VERSUS PRODUCT AND PROCESS DEVELOPMENT

Although in the preceding discussion R&D has been treated as a single activity, the use of separate terms for research and development implies that there is a distinction between the two in the form of the activities and in their sequence in time. How much of each to build into the total program and when in the R&D life cycle each is important are significant factors in the time dimension of R&D management.

It is important first that the R&D manager realize that there is no distinction in financial reporting between research and development (FASB 2). Thus, annual reports combine the two into a single numerical value. Surveys based on financial reporting also give only a sum of R&D for each of many companies in an industry (*Business Week*).

In the title of this section, the terms *advanced technology* and *applied research* have been used to capture the intent of work which is properly within the scope of industrial research management. The decline of industrial support of basic research has been noted and deplored (Nason et al., 1978). Yet any serious consideration of the time value of money, as outlined in Chapter 2, makes living with the long time cycle of undirected basic research unappealing to industrial general management unless its sales potential is very high (Manners and Louderback, 1979). Thus, pioneering exploration and undirected research activities have a difficult life under the financial scrutiny of modern research management.

An impressive group of leaders of industrial research argue nevertheless for industry to sponsor investigations that require an intuitive departure from the present state of the art (Place, 1978). Though difficult to control and unpredictable in terms of results, this type of activity, properly directed, can be of major value to an industrial organization without large investments. Thus, an appropriate area of research activity for the industrial firm can be established in terms of specific bounds in certainty and effort required. When the certainty drops too low or the effort gets too large, the prudence of financial reward tempered by risk analysis sets limits on the level of activity in advanced technology and applied research.

Another set of limits comes from what a manufacturing department would call "buy versus make" analysis. To manufacture a part or subassembly requires more front-end investment than purchasing the equivalent item from a subcontractor, but it is hoped that manufacturing it will lower costs if volume is sufficiently high. With the large base of small entrepreneurial companies in North America, all but the very largest companies need to consider the extent to which they might buy parts of the products or processes they need rather than develop them themselves.

The R&D department under these conditions is often placed in the role of judge and jury with a large conflict of interest. Often only R&D has the technical expertise to qualify a subcontractor's component. Yet, "not invented here" is a natural reaction of the R&D manager's engineers, who would rather develop new products than qualify others from outside sources. The degree of certainty in either approach to acquiring a product often is equally low, yet the effort of qualification is appreciably lower than full product development, and this analysis must be undertaken as a management discipline.

Product and process development commence with a low degree of certainty since technical and commercial objectives are often set high with respect to the firm's initial base of knowledge. As efforts progress and as interim technical and cost objectives are met, the degree of certainty rises. Alternatively, to the extent that objectives cannot be met, projects are stopped in favor of ones whose certainty is rising.

The projects-started-to-projects-completed ratio often runs in excess of 20 for consumer products and 2 to 3 for industrial products.Prudent R&D management calls for early recognition of failure to meet technical objectives and resolute project terminations in the face of much pride of authorship by the project's engineering team. Even after technical objectives are achieved further commercial mortality occurs in the market development phase covered earlier in this chapter.

Quantitative approaches to successful R&D management will be covered in later chapters. To demonstrate the range of tradeoffs between advanced technology and applied research on the one hand and product development on the other, two qualitative examples will be discussed below.

Phi Instrumentation Company had moved progressively in the 1970s into more sophisticated electronic instrumentation systems based on minicomputer technology. At each point in time a new instrumentation system was proposed, a mapping of the proposed action was laid out as shown symbolically in Figure 4.2.

Certain elements were determined with little effort with a high degree of certainty. The functional specification could be quickly reduced to instructions per second and memory size requirements, which narrowed the choice of microprocessor to no more than three manufacturers' products. Actually while the certainty was high (about 90%), it was equally predictable that there was a high risk of some elements of functionality not fitting in the final design.

Algorithms could be specified with nearly the same high certainty and nearly the same low effort. Yet again, there was a high risk of some algorithms not working owing to factors such as noise and drift caused by digital rounding errors.

At the other extreme of the advanced technology section's expertise, the introduction of sensors and actuators manufactured in house represented a much higher degree of effort and a lower degree of certainty that performance and cost result would be acceptable.

The certainty level of product development was predicted to rise as development progressed, and more effort was expanded. Typically, the decision to cease the efforts of the advanced technology section and to concentrate on development only was made when the certainties of both sections were in the same range—at that point, further pursuit of less certain advanced technology solutions appeared unattractive compared with rising development activity. The level of costs and a possible delay of product introduction were a contributing factor in the decision.

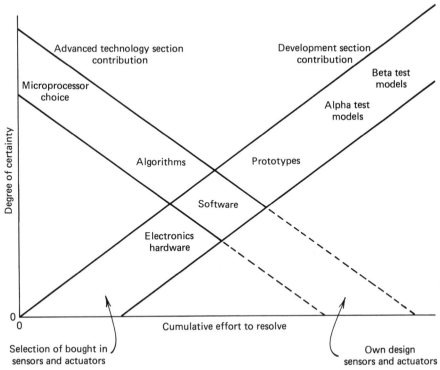

Figure 4.2.   Advanced technology versus development contribution

Another example covering a worldwide industry can be found in a survey of submarine telephone cable systems (Commerce Department, 1975).

Advanced technology proceeded from the vacuum tubes of the 1950s to transistorized repeaters (amplifiers) in the 1960s. At the same time cable technology went from cables with copper outer conductors to lighter-weight designs with aluminum outer conductors.

Within each generation of technology, product development began with short-haul systems of small capacity leading to long-haul systems of larger capacity, and so on. Within each technology generation, a family of sizes was ultimately developed by each ongoing manufacturer.

As of this writing, all surviving manufacturers are struggling with still another technology generation based on optical fiber cables with repeaters of optical and electronic devices. Survival in this industry has required both an advanced technology base to be ready to capitalize on the generational shifts in technology, and a product development capability to match the technology to varying traffic demands on a mixture of routes of differing distances.

Table 4.1. Percentage Allocation of R&D Expenses

Activity	Large Firms (%)	All Firms (%)	Small Firms (%)
Basic research	5.3	3.7	1
Applied research	28.6	22.0	9
Development	66.1	74.3	90

Sources. Large firms: Nason et al; 1978 (1975 expenses); all firms: NSF, 1976 (1975 expenses); small firms: author's estimates of a typical firm.

DISTRIBUTION OF THE RESEARCH AND DEVELOPMENT TIME CYCLE

The discussion of the research and development time cycle in this section assumes that a decision has been made between the conflicting goals of advanced technology and applied research and product and process development, and that the order of magnitude of research-type activities is in line with the averages indicated in Table 4.1.

The advanced technology and applied research activities in an industrial company tend to fall into three sets of activities: exploration and pioneering, screening and feasibility studies; and business analysis for project selection. This is then followed by product development, which is the largest activity in the development phase shown in Table 4.1. Other development activities are process and manufacturing development, testing, and commercialization. The whole cycle is shown graphically in Figure 4.3.

Exploration and Pioneering

Exploration and pioneering are the principal activities of research, whether defined as basic or applied or any of the other dozen modifications of the term *research* used in the literature (Sandretto, 1968, pp. 16–17). Research is the expenditure of technical effort to obtain new knowledge and the application of this knowledge, if not to specific products, to the general technology base applicable to the industrial firms' business mission.

Many studies have been made of actual cases of technological innovation, and any of these could have been used to illustrate the steps in the sequence of the R&D life cycle. The technology of fiber

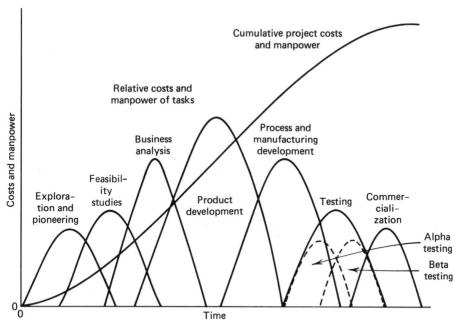

Figure 4.3. Distribution of the research and development time cycle

optics for the transmission of information is an example of a discontinuous innovation with which the author has personal knowledge and that is well documented in the literature (Pastelis, 1981).

Since the time of the glass blowers of medieval Venice, it has been known that slender fibers of glass can carry light, but with appreciable reductions in intensity over distances of a few centimeters. ITT's Kao, in 1964, was inspired to try to define the exact conditions under which a fiber of glass (or its base constituent, silica) clad with a covering of the same material of a different index of refraction could potentially have low losses over distances of tens of kilometers.

The consequent exploratory research focused not only on refining the system concept, but also on the basic measurement techniques needed for such low losses in short fibers, causes of the losses, processes for fabrication, and suitable light sources. At the beginning, only light detectors were sufficiently developed that exploration was unnecessary.

Similar exploration and pioneering was begun at AT&T's Bell Laboratories and at Corning Glass, plus many other locations. However, of the first 200 patents issued in the United States, about 30% each were to these two organizations and to ITT.

It was Corning's Maurer who had the intuition to abandon traditional crucible-based glass. Instead, he favored the chemical depositing
of silica from silicon-rich vapors to make the fibers, thus first achieving
the necessary degree of purity and the required control of the index
of refraction transition between core and cladding. Kao and Maurer
were awarded the prestigious Ericsson Prize in 1979 for their achieve-
ments.

Screening and Feasibility Studies

Often technology that is developed in a search for new knowledge
becomes a solution looking for a problem. Screening technology resulting from one's own applied research and that periodically an-
nounced in scientific articles is another phase of the R&D life cycle.
Like the creator of a new variety of fruit, the R&D manager must
look for a sturdy part of the company's organization tree onto which
to graft the new creation. Graftability and time in which to accomplish it become key decisions in industrial research. If no grafting
point is readily apparent the project may stay and grow in the advanced technology group or research laboratory until it is too large
or too late for successful exploitation by a product development team
in a profit and loss operation.

The mechanism by which advanced technology and applied research gets "marketed" to downstream product development organizations is the feasibility study. As with any invention, the research team must transform a concept into a tangible model. This
model must be documented with sufficient engineering data, including speculative costs, to permit the evaluation of feasibility by
the part of the organization onto which it is to be grafted.

The foregoing is based on the tacit assumption that most advanced
technology and applied research efforts will be focused on existing
markets or straightforward extensions thereof. The degree of certainty is low enough on a new product for an existing market, without aiming research efforts at new products for new markets. Nonetheless, a small fraction of new product/new market concepts will
surface in the best-managed R&D departments. When they do, the
thoroughness of the feasibility study needs to be even higher, as
many difficult questions will be asked by general management before
proceeding further. The potential for grafting onto an ongoing business in this case is reduced, and a new business unit may have to
be established to take the new technology through to innovation.

For AT&T and ITT, fiber optics was not seen as a new market, but as a discontinuity of technology in their existing markets for cables. Feasibility studies in both organizations were commenced in the late 1960s, as it became obvious that exploratory efforts were making progress. The losses per kilometer of fiber had dropped several orders of magnitude, although much still had to be done. Experiments had confirmed that the high information capacity needed was potentially realizable. Light sources (lasers) had been fabricated with the required characteristics and lives of tens of hours. An initial understanding of failure mechanisms gave an increased certainty of sufficiently long life for the product.

The principal focus of these studies was on obtaining an installable, spliceable, repairable cable of multiple fibers, as opposed to the single laboratory fibers then available. This meant also converting the early chemical vapor deposition lab apparatus to preproduction process machinery. At the same time production feasibility was needed for long-life lasers.

Business Analysis

Once the feasibility study is complete, or nearly so, a short but necessary business analysis phase usually takes place. In some cases, business analysis is done for short stretches during the feasibility phase. More often, once the feasibility report is prepared, the organizational unit designated to exploit the product begins to take the project seriously. A good business analysis effort requires the collaboration of the advanced technology team and the receiving organization's product management and development management, or senior individuals designated for the analysis effort from each department.

The essence of business analysis is the quantification of potential rewards weighed against potential costs and risks. Product management must obtain sufficient information about performance and functionality to make a preliminary analysis of possible sales. Product development must understand how much remains to be done and what technical risks are outstanding so that it can determine potential development costs. In all organizational sizes, as can be seen from Table 4.1, much more remains to be spent in development than has been expended to date in advanced technology and applied research. General management needs to be convinced that continuing with the project makes financial sense. Many tools, considered in detail in the next chapter, are available for project selection and analysis.

The timing of the business analysis phase of optical fibers at ITT was somewhat modified by an overall business analysis of all product lines for the decade of the 1970s called Project 80. Thus, a number of targets were accelerated, in advance of the original schedule for completion of the feasibility study effort, and subsequently refined in annual budget preparation.

The business analysis showed favorable results from continuing the project. A product development division was selected in the United States with strong electro-optic technology capability, but for whom fiber optic cables were both a new product and new market. For a variety of reasons, product development for the United Kingdom was continued in the research laboratories, pending establishment of a new business unit. Only in West Germany was the technology assigned to the cable division, for whom it was an existing market.

Product Development

To the development engineer for whom product development is the source of job satisfaction, the preliminaries often can be frustrating, as can the subsequent stages of process and manufacturing development, testing, and commercialization covered in later sections of this chapter. The reality, however, is that product development, as shown graphically in Figure 4.3, is only the middle third to one-half of the R&D time cycle, as measured by both effort and the passage of time.

Even the product development phase has tasks that are not strictly development as viewed by the engineer. The marketing/functional specification must be thoroughly analyzed and hardware design specifications prepared at the start of the project. If there is a microprocessor portion, software design specifications need to be prepared as well. The point is that development of a product is a disciplined task moving at a measured pace from what the marketing department considers the customer will find of value through me-

By the early 1970s, initial product specifications had been developed by ITT in the United States for military applications, and in the United States, the United Kingdom, and West Germany for commercial telecommunications applications. In all cases the specifications were for optical fiber cables, and the light source and detector subsystems were supposed to work with already existing digital terminal equipment designed originally for wire cables.

ticulous specification and equally meticulous design to that specification, and to target costs, so that the end product will have the
highest likelihood of being a technical and commercial success.

Process and Manufacturing Development

The extent of process and/or manufacturing development needed
varies with the specific product. In many cases, the product and
process are inseparable, and so a large effort must be mounted in
parallel with or closely behind product development.

In the past, as was the case with Bell Laboratories and Western
Electric in the first half of this century, product development was
completed and the product released before manufacturing development began. Bell Laboratories, departments are now located in
the same factories as Western Electric's manufacturing engineering,
and substantial overlap occurs. Under competitive pressure most
industries have instituted the overlap of product and process development shown graphically in Figure 4.3.

It is vital that the process and/or manufacturing development focus
on the realities of the factory within which the product will be made.
For a company with strong central control, the process work may
take place as far upstream as the central research laboratories (the
Olin Corporation's Metal Research Laboratories in New Haven, CT
are an example). This reduces the freedom of action of the plant
manager and places strong demands on the research manager. The
alternative often involves the extra cost of multiple process or manufacturing developments.

ITT as a long decentralized company has always found it difficult
to avoid duplication of manufacturing development. In the case of
optical fibers, the selection in the United States of a recipient division
strong in electro-optical technology virtually ensured the activity
would parallel that in Europe.

The United Kingdom and West German operations stayed together
longer because of the initially lower sophistication of the West German
cable division. However, by the mid 1970s, the needs of its factory
produced a divergence, particularly as the United Kingdom activity
was held in place at the research laboratory. Close coordination among
the three locations moved ideas among countries, but at a cost disadvantage compared with the centrally controlled competition.

Testing

Testing is the process by which what the development engineer has done is compared with the needs of the marketplace. This statement, made from a general manager's viewpoint, will bring spirited rebuttal from many R&D managers and from almost all quality control managers. They will insist that product qualification means compliance with the functional and design specifications.

Certainly, if the functional and design specifications were flawless, this latter viewpoint would hold. Flawless functional and design specifications, however, imply a degree of certainty at the start of the development which the author has rarely seen. Yet, to let product managers or development managers freely bend such specifications is to invite chaos.

If a product manager is not held to his original functional specification, the development manager is presented with a steadily moving target, which results in a disease known as "creeping elegance." If the development manager is not held to his design specifications, control is lost over the development process, and products may not be technically successful. If no specification is available, the quality control manager has no objective measure against which to qualify the product.

A practical resolution of this dilemma, when both product and development managers see that 100% certainty cannot be obtained in the time and budget allowed, is to draft still another specification for the product incorporating the maximum practical standards from the earlier specifications, and to test against the final product specification. If such a specification cannot be agreed to by marketing and R&D department heads, the project should be terminated.

The stage of testing to a product specification is often called alpha testing. It should be supervised or audited by quality control. A log should be kept of noncompliance together with actions taken to resolve, fix, and requalify noncomplying elements, or to accept them as a product limitation. The log should also record that the specification is rectified once and only if marketing considers the change in the product acceptable. It is a fact of life, however, that even successful alpha testing does not ensure that the product meets the needs of the marketplace. People who know the product well from its development phase are rarely clever enough to figure out how a customer will use (or misuse) the product in his own environment.

For this reason, a second set of tests is usually made called beta testing. Selected customers are invited to try the product in their installations provided they promise to report faithfully any problems they encounter. The same log kept for alpha testing should also be done for beta testing. As mentioned earlier in the chapter, this phase of the R&D life cycle initiates the introductory phase of the product life cycle.

Commercialization

The final phase of development is often called commercialization. Perhaps a better term is "mop up." Some of the necessary cleanup may include the following:

Release manufacturing information.
Release final product specification to marketing.
Prepare customer instructions and release.
Make marketing demonstration models.
Release alpha and beta test reports.
Release production software and firmware.
Participate in demonstrations until marketing is up to speed.
Participate in training until instructors are up to speed.
Support factory testing until production is running.

It is important for the R&D manager to consider commercialization as a human communication process. That is, it is complete not when his department sends it, but when the downstream departments receive and understand what has been released to them.

The first ITT fiber optic information transport systems were released, commercialized, and into customer installations in 1975 in the United States and the United Kingdom, and the following year in West Germany. The 11 to 12 year R&D life cycle from invention to innovation was not far from the mean for discontinuous innovations. Fiber optic communication systems are now well into the growth phase of the product life cycle and product line extensions have been introduced repeatedly by the many competitors now active in the field (Horsley, 1980).

SUMMARY AND CONCLUSION

This chapter has discussed the time dimension of R&D projects. Product life cycles have phases from introduction through market development, growth, maturity, and saturation. Either product line extensions are properly planned and successful, or products eventually enter a decline phase.

Research and development are differing aspects of R&D with differing goals. In industrial research, a certainty-versus-effort barrier limits how far into advanced areas management is willing to invest given the time value of money. Development programs increase in certainty with time and dominate R&D expenditure in firms of all sizes, or are judged as unable to meet goals and are terminated. For R&D programs that go on to completion, the phases are exploration, feasibility, business analysis, product development, process or manufacturing development, testing, and commercialization.

Some interesting generalizations come from this analysis. First, if the combination of R&D andproduct cycles is worth doing, it must be done correctly. If the price of doing the combined cycle right is too high for the potential reward, run, not walk, to the nearest exit. Second, costs increase exponentially in the early part of a project. Staying with losers too long absorbs much of the effort that could be devoted to screening potential winners. Finally, the kinds of risks that management must take with technological discontinutities are often the difference between survival and ruin. If this sounds somewhat like gambling, perhaps it is. It is the outlay today of hard-earned cash in the expectation of success in the far-from-certain future. Increasing the likelihood of success in such ventures is the challenge of project selection covered in the next chapter.

REFERENCES

Block, Robert G., "Ten Commandments for New Product Development", *Industrial Research/Development*, March 1979, 97–100.

Booz-Allen & Hamilton, *Management of New Products*, New York, 1975. *Business Week*, July 5, 1982, 54–74.

Butler, O.B., "What Marketing Expects from R&D", *Research Management*, **17** (6): 7–9 (1974).

Commerce Department of the United States, Office of Telecommunications, *The World's Submarine Telephone Cable Systems*, OT Contractor Report 75–2, Washington, D.C.: Government Printing Office, August 1975.

Dodson, Edward N., "Technological Change and Cost Analysis of High Technology Systems," *IEEE Transactions on Engineering Management*, **EM-24** (2): 38–45 (1977).

Financial Accounting Standards Board, *Statement of Financial Accounting Standards No. 2 (FASB 2)—Accounting for Research and Development Costs*, Stamford, CT: October, 1974.

Foster, Richard N., "Boosting the Payoff from R&D," *Research Management*, **25** (1): 22–27 (1982).

Gibson, John E., *Managing Research and Development*, New York: Wiley, 1981.

Gluck, Frederick W., Richard N. Foster, and John C. Forbis, "Cure for Strategic Malnutrition," *Harvard Business Review*, **54** (6): 154–165, (1976).

Horsley, A. W., and E. S. Usher, "Optical Fiber Communication Systems in PTT Networks," *Electrical Communication*, **55** (4); 268–275 (1980).

Levitt, Theodore, "Exploit the Product Life Cycle," *Harvard Business Review*, **43** (6): 81–94 (1965).

Levitt, Theodore, "Marketing Myopia", *Harvard Business Review*, **53** (5): 26–48 (1975).

Manners, George E., Jr., and Joseph G. Louderback, "Sales Potential Guidelines for Research Investment," unpublished monograph, Troy, NY: Rensselaer Polytechnic Institute, 1979.

Nason, Howard K., Joseph A. Steger, and George E. Manners, Jr., *Support of Basic Research by Industry*, St. Louis, MO: Industrial Research Institute Research Corporation, 1978.

National Science Foundation, *National Patterns of R&D Resources: Funds and Manpower in the United States, 1953–1977*, NSF 77-310, Washington, D.C.: Government Printing Office, 1977.

Pastelis, Anthony and George Stubbs, "Fiber-Optic Techniques Work Well," *Telecommunications*, **15** (12): 16–28 and 69–74 (1981).

Place, Geoffrey, "Wanted: Dionysians," *Chemtech*, August 1978, 458–462.

Sandretto, Peter C., *The Economic Management of Research and Engineering*, New York: Wiley, 1968.

White, William, "A Risk/Action Model for the Differentiations of R and D Profiles," *IEEE Transactions on Engineering Management*, **EM-29** (3): 88–93 (1982).

Wood, Edward C., *Case Studies on the Process of Technological Innovations in the Economy's Private Sector*, Menlo Park, CA: Stanford Research Institute, 1975.

5

PROJECT SELECTION AND EVALUATION

The most critical strategic issue facing research directors and general managers is maximizing the profit contribution made over time by the firm from its decisions to invest in research and development (Foster, 1982).

INTRODUCTION

One of the most difficult tasks of a multiproduct business is the selection and evaluation of new R&D projects. It should be realized that these projects are of the same nature as any investment in the future of the business; that is, they represent an outlay of cash today in the expectation of a greater return in the risk-filled future. Many factors are part of project selection that are not purely financial, including the hopes and fears of marketing people as well as the judgments of technical people about which technologies will be survivors.

Because project selection and evaluation is so difficult, it appears desirable to make a thorough review of its many facets. These include the problems and emotions involved in subjective assessments; the types of risks involved according to the degree of newness in the technology and marketplace; the advantages and problems of a number of methods of objective assessment; financial hurdles for objective assessments; and the need for discretionary projects to ensure sound decisions when inputs are missing from the decision-making process.

SUBJECTIVE ASSESSMENTS

Much emotion tends to surround the project selection activity. A number of the excuses encountered during project justification are: (1) "This product is needed to round out our product line." (2) "Our competitors have this product." (3) "Our competitors will come out with this product in six months; if we can't meet them, we will be out of business." (4) "This product has to be modified to have the magic bullet of reliability (or other element of functionality)." (5) "Our salesmen already call on the same customers."

Many similar excuses could be added to the list with the degree of emotional intensity in the statement usually reflecting the degree of difficulty in justifying the product on any criteria other than hunch (Carley, 1982). For the individual entrepreneur it may well be that his track record on subjective assessment is sufficiently high for him to proceed on this basis. For most rational businesses, however, it is clearly necessary to have some more objective guidelines. These guidelines are needed not only to keep technical and marketing people honest but, also, to satisfy the natural inclination of any business to want advance notice as to the quantitative financial impact on the bottom line of any cash outlay as a precondition for making it.

It is particularly important to structure objective assessments in the manner that is natural for the financial reviewer. Regardless of the differences in accounting treatment, the financial hurdles have long since been established for capital appropriations. To use different figures and different methodology for project selection and evaluation tends not to put the potential high returns of new product development in a proper reference frame with respect to capital appropriations for extensions of capacity for current products.

PROJECT SELECTION RISKS

Before moving to methods of objective setting, the degree of risk of certain courses of action needs to be assessed in terms that match financial ones.

It is widely recognized in portfolio management that a premium in return should be expected that is directly proportional to the increment of risk above a prospective riskless investment. (In the United States, the going rate on 90 day Treasury bills is, usually, taken as the measure of a riskless investment, for if the government were to default, any measurement in financial terms would be invalid anyway).

The continuation of existing products in any company represents a more risky endeavor than investng in, for example, Treasury bills. This already establishes a frame of reference for prospective financial hurdles. The measurement of risk in this case is the amount by which the anticipated profit is likely to vary based on the changing conditions of the economic cycle. Any course of action other than continuing existing products in existing markets entails some additional risks. These additional risks are considered below in three categories:

1. Enhanced or value-analyzed products
2. New products for existing markets
3. New products for new markets

Enhancing, or value analyzing, existing products has both low technical and commercial risks. This type of "tail-fin engineering" produces relatively predictable volumes of business for the technical effort involved and the relatively certain product costs since the existing product should have been costed to a fair degree of accuracy. Thus, these products can be considered nearly the same as existing products in terms of setting financial objectives, with a, perhaps, modest risk premium corresponding to the degree of enhancement or change involved.

The Iota Division had been manufacturing a form of electronic multiplex since the early 1930s. Consequently, it knew both the domestic and international markets and prices, probable competition reactions, and probable upper and lower limits to sales volume. In 1967, it knew that a 1970 product introduction was required of a new model, that its cost (in constant dollars) had to be 24% lower than the current model, reflecting a traditional 8% a year reduction in real cost of the product, and that current technology using new components could achieve that cost level. The development project was both a technical and commercial success.

New products for existing markets have a higher technical risk because much less is known in advance of the prospective cost of the product, and engineers without experience in cost techniques can often be optimistic about both product and development costs. On the other hand, if the markets are truly existing markets, the degree of commercial risk is low because the existing marketing force may be assumed capable of making reasonable judgments not only about customers' prospective purchases but, also, about the possible responses of competitors, whose behavior they will have already observed. It is important in this regard that existing markets be ones where the customers are present ones and the competitors are present ones. If the customers are the same but the new product moves into a bracket where a significantly different competitor group is likely to be established, it is less likely that the marketing force will be able to anticipate competitor reaction, and the product should be considered one for a new market.

A new product for a new market has both high technical risks and high commercial risks. The high technical risks are the same as in the evaluation of product and development costs for any new products. The increases in commercial risks come not only from

The same Iota Division, in 1972, determined that an additional new model was required in 1976. The uncertainty of markets and prices was no higher, and a new cost target was forecast based on traditional trends. Engineering, however, believed a change to a new technology was required to meet the cost target. This risk was not factored into the project's approval, and the development proceeded. The product met its performance objectives, but was high in cost because of the unfamiliar technology. This lost some export market share, as competitors had successfully brought out new models in the older technology. This loss of forecast volume further raised product costs. The product was saved from being a financial problem only because domestic market acceptance was high, despite the higher price needed to cover costs.

competitor reactions but, also, from the strong probability that existing competitors will be further down the experience curve than one's own company. This advantage gives competitors higher margins during the product competition, or for more intense promotion, or both wich puts the new entrant at a disadvantage.

One is forced to conclude that whatever financial hurdle has been established for existing products for existing markets needs to be increased under the three conditions indicated above. Each company must try to assess what these risk premiums should be in terms of their knowledge of the characteristics of their markets. In the author's experience, enhanced or value-analyzed products need between 0 and 5% higher return; new products for existing markets need 5 to 10% higher return; and new products for new markets need 15 to 25% higher return than is needed to maintain the business with existing products for existing markets.

OBJECTIVE ASSESSMENTS

A number of different types of objective assessment techniques have been devised from time to time. These include sales volume, sales-to-development ratio, cash flow payback, net present value, benefit-to-cost ratio, and internal rate of return.

Because internal rate of return, or discounted cash flow rate of return, is used in many companies' capital expenditure control procedures, it has been used as a common yardstick for considering the validity of some of the other means of objective assessment. The IRR, or DCFRR, is the discount rate at which the total cash flow (capital cost and future income) is discounted to a present value of zero. In other words, it is the rate at which the present value of a capital cost outflow equals the present value of future profit inflows.

In project selection and evaluation from a conceptual standpoint (but not from an accounting one), the development cost of a project needs to be considered in the same manner as capital. Because accounting directly expenses development costs in the current accounting period, it does not matter whether the calculations are made on a before or after tax basis, as long as the same basis is used for both development expense and future profits.

Incremental Sales Volume

The concept of incremental sales volume is very popular in the marketing community because it meets their commercial objectives to go for the highest order input. A ranking of projects by sales volume, however, does not register the effects of the costs associated with each of the various projects. It is entirely possible, for example, that a series of smaller projects using less resources proportionately per project could result in a higher financial return to the company, even though it may be more difficult for marketing to handle multiple products than to handle a single one.

In addition, the use of incremental sales volume does not result in a reasonable scheme for rationing scarce development resources.

Sales-to-Development Ratio

A study was made a few years ago in an attempt to relate the value of a development to important factors in its cost (Gilman, 1978). The author developed the following formula for the value of a development:

$$\text{VALUE} = \frac{E}{D}\left[\frac{(1+g)^{t-t_0} - 1}{g(1+i)^t}\right]$$

where E = first-year earnings
$\quad\quad\ D$ = development cost
$\quad\quad\ g$ = growth rate in earnings

$$i = \text{interest rate}$$
$$t = \text{time after start of development}$$
$$t_0 = \text{delay between development and first-year earnings}$$

This formula leads to the conclusion that value is maximized by a high ratio of first-year earnings to development costs, a high earnings growth rate that is greater than the interest rate, and a minimum delay between development and first-year earnings.

To the extent that this model is appropriate to the projects in hand, it provides a good initial rating system. However, earnings calculations tend to be somewhat more difficult in the early stages of a project. Also, earnings rarely grow constantly.

On the average, the rate of earnings to sales in most businesses tends toward a traditional level. Thus, the use of sales as a proxy for earnings is a convenient early screening technique.

Kappa Division used a sales-based screening technique in 1970. It was based only on the first three-years sales forecasts and was somewhat optimistic in its inventory assumptions so that SDR values were conservative and calculated IRR values were optimistic. Table 5.1 and Figure 5.1 show the results of screening seven projects. The payback data in Table 5.1 will be considered in the next section.

Table 5.1. Kappa Division Sales-to-Development Ratio as a Forecaster of Internal Rate of Return and Payback, 1970

Project	Development cost ($,000)	Three-years sales ($,000)	Sales-to-development ratio	IRR (%)	Years payback
Relay modification	34	2,268	66.7	100.0	1.7
Solid state relay	71	998	14.0	48.9	2.4
Thermal relay	120	2,362	19.7	54.1	2.7
Nickel relay	34	765	22.5	50.2	2.4
Tele relay	173	2,004	11.6	36.3	3.4
Relay control	564	7,962	14.1	28.9	3.8
Relay extensions	53	1,520	28.7	31.3	3.9

Source: Adapted by author from proprietary data.

IRR significant at the 1% level (r = 0.87). Costs and IRR are on an operating basis before interest and federal income taxes.

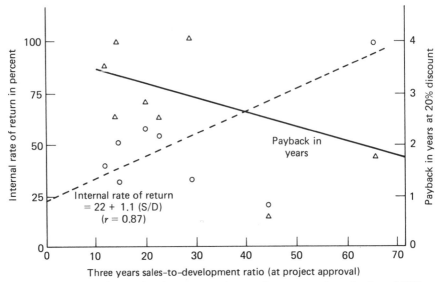

Figure 5.1. Sales-to-development ratio as a forecaster of payback and IRR

Table 5.2. Kappa Division Sales-to-Development Ratio Versus Internal Rate of Return (1976)

Project	Development cost ($000)	Three-years sales ($000)	Sales-to-development ratio	IRR (%)
New relay control	956	1,920	2	19.0
New S.S. relay	505	1,530	3	19.0
Tele relay mod.	398	2,810	7	22.5
Silver relay	51	355	7	25.5
Gold relay	48	350	7	36.0
Relay mod.	46	370	8	25.0
Reed relay	490	4,400	9	33.2
Gravity relay	210	2,150	10	30.0
Delay relay	145	1,465	10	33.5
New armature	98	1,400	14	40.0
Material change	105	3,190	31	73.0

Source: Adapted by author from proprietary data.

IRR significant at 1% level (r = 0.97). Costs and IRR are on an operating basis before interest and federal income taxes.

Based on the small sample of Table 5.1, Figure 5.1 shows graphically the ratio of the first three years of sales to the cost of development. Trend lines are calculated by least squares. The ground
rules in effect in 1970 were somewhat optimistic because of underlying assumptions giving an optimistic formula for the trend line.
However, it can be seen from Figure 5.1 that a good correlation had
been established on these older projects between the sales-to-development ratio and return, which indicates that this ratio is a reasonable forecaster of profitability.

In 1976, in the same division, a number of new projects were costed through the use of a more realistic inventory criterion. Again, a
high correlation was established between the sales-to-development
ratio and the IRR, albeit at a lower level of return than the previous
trend owing to the change in assumptions. The data are summarized
in Table 5.2 and shown graphically in Figure 5.2. Again, a linear

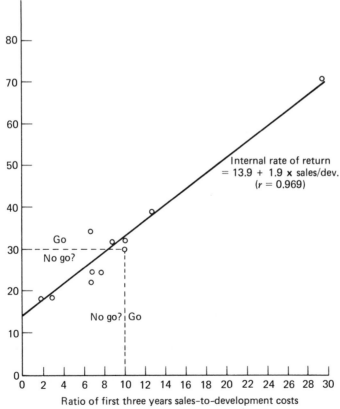

Figure 5.2.   Internal rate of return versus sales-to-development ratio

correlation appears between the IRR and the sales-to-development ratio, with a correlation coefficient significant at the 1% level. The values of internal rate of return are comparable with alternate investments at that time in the division. The dotted lines indicate approximately where the cutoff points were placed by general management after considering alternative investment opportunities.

The conclusion of this exercise is that the sales-to-development ratio is a good early screening tool for project selection and evaluation. However, to be theoretically correct, it fails to consider the time value of money, as in the Gilman model. In addition, it presupposes a constant relationship of sales to earnings, which is, perhaps, an unwarranted assumption.

Cash Flow Payback

Cash flow payback can be defined as the time required to recover an investment out of future earnings. In the procedure used in the Kappa Division in 1970, shown in Figure 5.1 and Table 5.1, this payback was specifically measured from the date of market introduction, under the assumption that all cash outflow and inflow were discounted at a 20% annual rate. Other assumptions would change the payback period. The calculation is shown graphically in Figure 5.3.

The calculation of cash flow payback is not a very sophisticated approach. It ignores the product life after the payback period, which in some businesses can be substantial. It ignores the market introduction characteristics that may traditionally be slow because of a conservative industry.

Despite these shortcomings an investigation of the same Kappa Division projects in Figure 5.1 (plus three value analysis projects also of the same vintage) on a linear relationship showed a high negative linear correlation between internal rate of return and years of payback, shown in Figure 5.4. This correlation is significant at the 1% level.

An investigation of theoretical models shows that at high rates of return and long years of payback, a reciprocal relationship should exist between IRR and payback. The truth of this may be seen by dividing the present value of an annuity by its periodic rate, the equivalent of the calculation of payback on an actual project. But the present value PV is equal to the periodic rate R times the annuity factor for the number of years n at the interest rate i.

The formula for this annuity factor is as follows:

$$A_{n/i} = \frac{1 - (1 + i)^{-n}}{i} \tag{1}$$

where i is the interest rate and n is the number of years over which interest is earned (presumably greater than the payback years). Thus, it may be seen that at high interest rates and/or long periods of return, the payback may be approximated as the reciprocal of the interest rate. This rule of thumb was tested for the same set of data and, indeed, as also shown in Figure 5.4, a higher correlation coefficient is found for this reciprocal relationship, significant well in excess of 1% level.

Thus, although payback is not a good guide for long-life projects, it does have a clear relationship to the internal rate of return when a number of projects in the same industry are considered. One of its biggest shortcomings is that it is liable to be interpreted subjec-

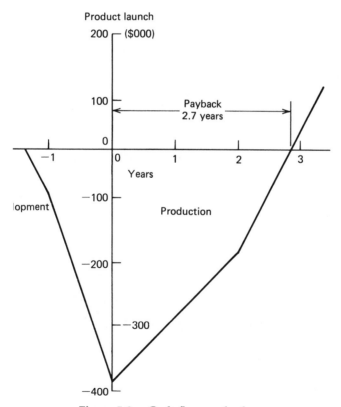

Figure 5.3. Cash flow payback

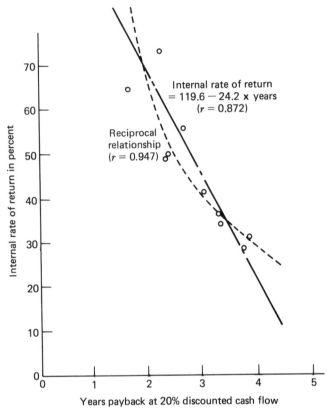

Figure 5.4. Internal rate of return versus years payback

tively with the comment: "Two years is too long for a payback," in spite of the fact that because of the characteristics of the product and the served market, the project may be very valuable.

Net Present Value

Net present value is defined as the algebraic sum of all cash flows discounted at the company's agreed hurdle rate (hurdle rates are discussed in a subsequent section). Projects should be accepted if their net present value is positive. This is a theoretically accurate means of screening projects, and often adopted in the capital and value analysis procedures.

The principal problem with net present value is that there is not a good method for ranking projects under rationing. A large project may have a large net present value and still not be as good for the company as the sum of a larger number of smaller projects, each with individually smaller, positive net present values.

Benefit-to-Cost Ratio

This objective assessment method was largely developed in the govenmental sector as the ratio of the money value of returns of a project to the project's cost. Its proper use requires the factoring in of the time value of money, which is usually done by discounting to the agreed-on hurdle rate. A moment of reflection will reveal that a benefit-to-cost ratio of one corresponds to a net present value and an internal rate of return of zero. Figure 5.5, derived from the Lambda Division's products, shows the relationship between internal rate of return and the ratio of return to outlay (benefit–cost ratio). This curve was derived with a one year delay between the end of development and product introduction. A shorter introduction period would create a more vertical curve, and a longer one a flatter curve.

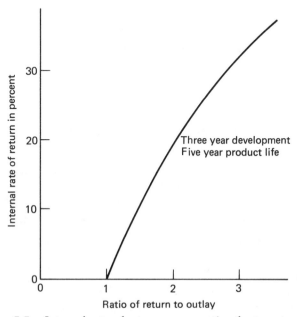

Figure 5.5. Internal rate of return versus ratio of return to outlay

Benefit-to-cost ratio is a good indicator of project value with the same theoretical base of net present value and a direct relationship to internal rate of return. It also provides a more than adequate means of ranking projects so that the projects to be done initially should be those of the highest benefit-to-cost ratio.

Internal Rate of Return

As noted in the above subsections, internal rate of return directly relates to other objective assessment methods and permits easy comparison not only of value analysis with new products but, also, with capital expenditure decisions. IRR is available on a number of pocket calculators and easy to program on office computers. Thus, it is a very practical tool for project evaluation.

The principal theoretical fault of IRR is that it assumes reinvestment of all cash flows at its own rate. Therefore, the value to the company of any very high IRR is overstated. Despite this, its ease of use and ability to communicate with the financial fraternity makes the IRR a preferred method for future objective assessments.

Some marketing organizations have proposed that some index should be undertaken that combines internal rate of return with incremental sales volume. Unless there is an excess level of development resources available for a long period of time to tackle new projects, such a revised index does not seem likely, especially since it would not compare favorably with the use of IRR alone, with its built-in suitability for setting project priorities as covered in the next section.

ACCEPTANCE CRITERIA

Virtually every company has identified a minimum acceptable rate of return for new capital expenditures. This rate is often called *the hurdle rate*, as mentioned previously. In an ideal world a company should be willing to undertake all capital projects whose return is higher than the hurdle rate. This hurdle rate is usually set at the weighted average cost to the company of incremental capital.

Given the premiums above this rate required for the risks described in an earlier section, and conceptual equivalency of product development and capital investment, a company, ideally, should undertake all projects for which the estimated internal rate of return exceeds its weighted average cost of capital, plus a risk premium according to the characteristic of the project. This is shown graphically by the Go/No Go? lines in Figure 5.2

Companies seldom do all projects that meet these criteria because they are constrained by one or more resources. Capital must be budgeted, and development resources are normally kept down by budget constraints in the interest of meeting certain profit objectives. Thus, an additional criterion is needed to ration projects within available resources.

The most practical procedure for rationing scarce development resources is to list projects in rank order by internal rate of return. If projects are in the early stage, tentative rate of return can be estimated from the sales-to-development ratio, as indicated in an earlier section. Starting with the highest internal rate of return, all projects should be undertaken that fit within the available resources, even though their prospective IRRs are well above the hurdle rate, and projects above the hurdle rate go undone. This is shown graphically in Figure 5.6.

Of course, if not enough projects fall on the list, the program should be stopped at the hurdle rate. Under this condition, brainstorming sessions for new products would appear a better investment than reducing the size of the development resources.

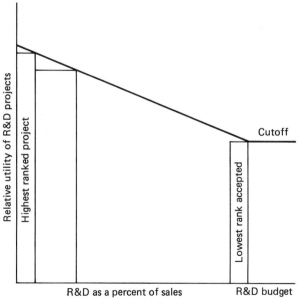

Figure 5.6. Typical R&D selection process. (From Ellis, 1980. Copyright Research Management.)

A final approach might be to consider the characteristics of projects according to a classification originally developed by Peter Drucker (used with permission of Harper & Row, 1964):

1. *Today's Breadwinners.* High revenue and high margin products are the backbone of today's business and of the successes of previous development programs.

2. *Tomorrow's Breadwinners.* These are the hope of today's development programs. Kappa Division's Thermal Relay (Table 5.1) fits this category.

3. *Productive Specialties.* Smaller-revenue-producing products with high returns fit this category. An example is Kappa Division's Nickel Relay (Table 5.1).

4. *Development Products.* Longer-range high-potential products fall into this category. The advanced development work at Kappa Division in 1970 (not shown in Table 5.1) led to the Reed Relay project of 1976 (Table 5.2).

5. *Failures.* An example of failure is the 1970 Relay Control project of the Kappa Division (Table 5.1) and its successor proposal in 1976 (Table 5.2), which did not get approved. Marketing myopia or technical obsolescence are two frequent causes (Levitt, 1975).

6. *Yesterday's Breadwinners.* Time has passed these by, but marketing still meets its order intake budget from enhancing them. Strict attention to profitability is required to avoid tying up scarce rsources supporting them. Kappa Division's Tele Relay Modification (Table 5.2) is an example of support mistakenly given to yesterday's breadwinner.

7. *Repair Jobs.* These are high potential projects with a fatal flaw that may be able to be fixed. Kappa Division's Solid State Relay (Table 5.2) clearly built upon the success of its predecessor (Table 5.1). Its development cost, however, was out of line because it was made to serve as a vehicle for the reeducation of technically obsolescent engineers. Cut to the lean approach of the earlier product, it moved into the productive specialty category.

8. *Unnecessary Specialties.* Most of these result from overcategorization at the request of marketing. Kappa Division's Nickel/Silver/Gold Relays fall into this category; an earlier program to develop a single family of corrosion-resistant relays as a potential productive specialty/breadwinner could have been more cost effective.

9. *Unjustified Specialties.* These are differentiations for which the customer will not pay. Kappa Division's screening process kept these out of the R&D program.

10. *Investments in Managerial Ego.* This harsh term of Peter Drucker's covers most projects supported only by subjective assessments (covered earlier in this chapter).

11. *Cinderellas or Sleepers.* The dream is always there that the next project will be a real winner if it gets support. The concern is that if not identified correctly, it will be undersupported, and the long time from the start to the completion of the development program will kill profitability.

The point of introducing the above classification scheme is to supplement the initial screening of objective assessments with a categorization that looks at projects differently. Often high functionality is demanded for a low sales forecast, which violates the KISS rule (that is, Keep It Simple, Stupid). If the modified projects still fail to pass the objective assessment hurdle, then they should be dropped from consideration.

In summary, research and development projects are in competition for the financial resources of a company. By selecting productive projects with internal rates of return above the cost of capital and a risk premium, the engineering manager is putting forward a good case to argue for his department.

DISCRETIONARY PROJECTS

Notwithstanding the financially oriented set of criteria for objective assessment elaborated in previous sections, it is necessary for an engineering department to have project money at its own discretion.

First, there is a basic problem of missing inputs. The product cost may not be known accurately enough to give a realistic input to an objective screening process. Marketing inputs may, similarly, be lacking. Also, in many instances there is a need to prove a critical technology before a project can be fully evaluated. The basic mechanism to solve the problem of missing inputs is to establish feasibility studies or similar discretionary projects. If sufficiently large, such discretionary projects may be established with a specific end goal in mind. On the other hand, there may be a need for a continuing project at an overhead level to which engineers can be assigned to investigate the bases for new products. Such continuing projects will avoid the need for formal approval for bright ideas of small monetary value and help encourage productivity and creativity among individual engineers.

Feasibility studies aimed at a specific product should be established with clear intermediate objectives in mind. The managers should ask: "What are the critical things that must be established before a more formal project evaluation can be done?" You must also ask: "How long will it take to achieve this fundamental knowledge, and what are realistic intermediate milestones?" Feasibility studies without the attendant disciplines of milestones and design reviews can often be money wasters.

A third reason for discretionary projects is to give visibility to bootlegging. Engineers will always find some way to investigate something that interests them. In the absence of discretionary projects, this bootlegging becomes an overhead cost or an excess direct charge on some convenient project where costs cannot be identified that exactly. In the writer's opinion, it has always been better to provide visibility to bootlegging to secure direction for creative work than to assume that it will never happen.

SUMMARY AND CONCLUSION

This chapter covered the problems and excuses of subjective assessments for project selection and evaluation, and concludes that there is a need for objective assessment. Risk premiums were identified for use in objective setting according to the degree of newness—both technically and commercially. Various types of objective assessments were viewed with the conclusion that the internal rate of return is a good objective assessment tool and easy to use with modern computers. A hurdle rate was recommended for an evaluation criterion equal to the company's cost of capital, plus a risk premium for newness. The handling of projects in conditions of limited resources was also covered. An argument was made for the use of discretionary projects to provide bases for new products and to solve problems of minimizing inputs for decision making. It is believed that by following thes principles, project selection and evaluation can be done on a more professional basis than in the past.

EXERCISES

New products in new markets make excellent topics for business school case studies and student learning through the case study method. Some selections are indicated below, all distributed by the Intercollegiate Case Clearing House, Soldier's Field, Cambridge, MA 02163.

Biggadike, Ralph, *Scott-Air Corporation*, No. 3-578-607.

Harvard Business School, *Gould Inc.—Graphics Division*, No. 9-571-071.

Harvard Business School, *Harlan Chemical Corporation*, No. 9-574-011.

REFERENCES

Albala, America, "Stage Approach for the Evaluation and Selection of R&D Projects," *IEEE Transactions on Engineering Management*, **EM-22** (4); 153–164 (1975).

Baker, Norman, and James Freeland, "Recent Advances in R&D Benefit Measurement and Project Methods," *Management Science*, **21** (10); 1164–1175 (1975).

Carley, William M., "Computer Wars: Were IBM's Tactics Against Control Data Unfair or Just Tough?," *Wall Street Journal*, May 19, 1982, 1 and 27.

Dohrmann, R. J., "Quantifying Contract Research Projects," *Research Management*, **25** (2): 30–33 (1982).

Drucker, Peter F., *Managing for Results*, New York: Harper & Row, 1964, 51.

Foster, Richard N., "Boosting the Payoff from R&D," *Research Management*, **25** (1): 22–27 (1982).

Gibson, John E., *Managing Research and Development*, New York: Wiley, 1981, Chapter 10.

Gilman, John J., "Factors that Affect Development Investment Values," *Research Management*, **21** (6): 22–23 (1978).

Gluck, Frederick W., Richard N. Foster, and John C. Forbis, "Cure for Strategic Malnutrition," *Harvard Business Review*, **54** (6): 154–165 (1976).

Jackson, Byron, "Decision Methods for Evaluating R&D Projects," *Research Management*, **26** (4):16–22 (1983).

Levitt, Theodore, "Marketing Myopia," *Harvard Business Review*, **53** (5): 26–48 (1975).

Manners, George E., Jr., and Joseph G. Louderback, "Sales Potential Guidelines for Research Investment," unpublished monograph, Troy, NY: Rensselaer Polytechnic Institute, 1979.

Merrifield, D. Bruce, "Selecting Projects for Commercial Success," *Research Management*, **24** (6): 13–18 (1981).

6

RISK AND UNCERTAINTY

In the previous chapter it was shown that the level of certainty tends to rise with the progress of development. Nevertheless, some consideration has to be given in the R&D management process to the lack of certainty. The absence of certainty is called risk by some authors and uncertainty by others.

In the realm of economic theory, the distinction between risk and uncertainty is often based on whether the probability distribution of outcomes is known or unknown (Quirin, 1967, p. 199). Where known distributions of outcomes can be calculated or inferred, the term *risk* is preferred since it represents a continuation of the principal thrust of this book toward quantification of the R&D investment process. Only for the residual cases where a nonprobabilistic distribution of outcomes is likely, or feared, will the term *uncertainty* be used. Methods of handling it are covered later in this chapter.

CONSIDERING RISK IN DECISIONS

Risks arise because of imperfect knowledge of the future. Estimates of development and product costs have inherent inaccuracies of a predictable and measurable sort. They may also be biased up or down owing to the frailties of human nature and/or weaknesses in the R&D management and control procedures. Except at points of great discontinuity, past experience in the firm or from the R&D manager's own career background elsewhere should serve to allow the dimensioning of the extent of risk in cost estimates.

On the other side of the decision equations are the estimates of benefits. Forecasts of future markets, market shares that indicate expected sales, and margins specifying rates of return are equally subject to variation. Except in start-up companies, it should be expected that past experience will also give some measurable dimensions to the extent of risks involved.

Even where past experience has not yet created a sound data base for the quantification of risk, modern techniques of simulation can often lead to more acceptable predictions of outcomes than were a measurement of risk not made at all.

The sources of risk can be classified in many ways. There are those external to the firm—the fluctuations of the marketplace and business cycle, the actions of competitors, and the initiatives of governmental agencies. From inside the firm there are the results of management decisions, past and present. Some internal risks are operating in nature causing fluctuations in net income before interest and taxes. Additional fluctuations arise from the ways in which the firm is financed since a large overhang in debt repayments can magnify the effect of operating variations.

Some internally generated risks can affect the survival of a business more critically than the technical risks involved in development. These derive from negative decisions to harvest certain products or to skimp on product safety and integrity, as well as from positive decisions involving forward or backward integration with implications for customer or supplier bases, respectively (Block, 1979).

Other classifications are the opportunity loss of benefits arising from innovations not made in time, losses of market from competitors' innovations, shifts in consumers' preferences, and changes in component and material prices or availability (Wood, 1975).

All of these classifications of the sources risk can be reduced to a common denominator—the potential for unforeseen variations up and down in predicted cash flows, both inward and outward. The financial director of a firm tends to be risk adverse since his concern is with the threat of bankruptcy from a succession of unexpectedly large negative cash flows. The individual entrepreneur and venture capitalist may be risk seeking and prepared to lose his small stake in the interest of potentially large returns if all goes according to or better than plan. The utility of risk to the supplier of funds is another factor that must be considered in decision making under risk conditions.

In today's world of quantitative management, therefore, the R&D manager must be prepared not only to consider risks in decision making, but also to place numerical values on the probable impact of those risks on cash flow assumptions used in project selection and evaluation. This is not to say that quantitative methodologies for risk determination should be the only necessary prerequisites for R&D management, although an appreciable body of management science focuses on such approaches (Perrakis and Sahin, 1976). This willingness of the R&D manager to be measured quantitatively has to be tempered with the realities of the difficulties of obtaining accurate data, the time and costs of doing so versus other opportunity costs confronting the R&D department, and the problems of using the risk measurements practically in project selection and evaluation schemes.

PROBABILITY DISTRIBUTION OF OUTCOMES

The future is never fully predictable, but within certain limits, a large fraction of human endeavor is based on the past. For example, senior section heads will have made numerous estimates in the past giving a base of data from which the probability distribution of newly made estimates can be inferred. The probable depth of business cycle recessions can be inferred from past recessions and the characteristics of the booms that have preceded them. Generally, wherever we have a base of knowledge of past outcomes, we may measure it with the techniques of statistical inference and obtain measures of bias, dispersion, and skewness that can be used to project future outcomes.

Consider the range of possible probability distributions of outcomes depicted in Figure 6.1. In the idealized case, with outcomes determined by pure chance fluctuations in estimates and with good R&D management, it could be expected that the mean of outcomes would be exactly the preestimated value and that the dispersion would be narrow about the mean. In this case, risk measured quantitatively would be low. The calculation of central tendency (mean) and dispersion (variance or standard deviation) is the subject of elementary statistical textbooks and is available on most computers and many hand calculators.

Still in the idealized case but with less-skilled R&D management, it could be expected that a bias toward higher-than-expected outcomes would be equivalent to a bias toward underestimates. In addition, a greater dispersion would also be expected. Again classical statistics applied to past outcomes allows assessment of risk in future estimates.

The problem with idealized distributions, in the author's experience, is that real distributions are not governed by chance, but are skewed because under "Murphy's Law," if something can go wrong, it will. The effect of this real-world tendency on the probability distribution is added costs to repair problems on a certain fraction of projects. Unfortunately, these costs are not miraculously offset when things go right. Thus, the distribution is one-tailed, skewed in the direction of the outcomes of a few projects greatly exceeding preestimates. This can be seen in the realistic cases of Figure 6.1. The good R&D manager keeps the peak of his distribution curve near the preestimate, but inadvertences keep a few projects in cost trouble, which in turn cause a shift in the mean of outcomes.

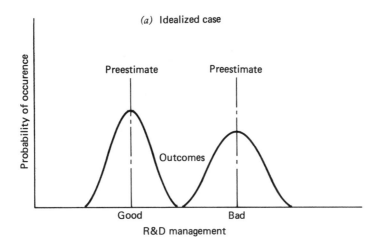

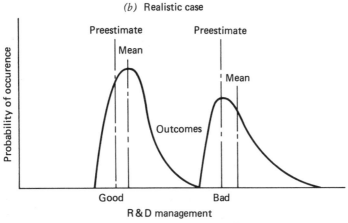

Figure 6.1.   Probability distribution of outcomes

Upsilon Radio Company introduced in 1952 a common cost system for development and customer application engineering projects. The latter tended to have a higher certainty than the former, so overall results were better than for the development sections alone. After running the costing system for a year to get section heads and managers fully familiar with it, a second year's results showed about 70% of projects below estimate (the lowest 12% below) and about 30% above estimate (the worst 55% over). The mean was 4% over estimate, and the standard deviation 21%. Thus, the worst project was within three standard deviations, but the standard deviation was not a valid measure for projects below estimate. Statistical measures of skewness were looked at but never built into the management scheme.

Naturally enough, the combination of poor R&D management and the problems of inadvertence produces in Figure 6.1 an even worse mean and dispersion than in the idealized case. Statistical methods may still be used in such cases until the tail of the distribution becomes so long that the methods become meaningless. The author has in the past atempted to salvage projects up to three times as costly as estimates and has seen factors of 10 documented (Brooks, 1976, pp. 278–280). These however, have to be considered special cases outside normal probability distributions A good working rule for applying statistical approaches is to check that the worst case project is within three standard deviations of the mean.

If we were to draw a chart equivalent to Figure 6.1 (b) for marketing estimates, net present value, internal rate of return, or benefit-to-cost ratio, most probably the tail of the distribution would be on the left. Marketing people are naturally reluctant to estimate much higher sales or profits than necessary to obtain project approval, and misjudgment or competitors' innovations tend to make large downside swings likely on a fraction of projects. Since the other measures combine benefits less (or divided by) costs, the tail tends to reflect the compounding of marketing and engineering outcome distributions.

As noted in the example above, a normalized measure of dispersion is a useful form for considering the probability distribution of outcomes. Mathematically, this is termed *the coefficient of variation* and is equal to the ratio of the standard deviation of a distribution to its expected value. If the distribution is not overskewed, the coefficient of variation may be a sufficient index of risk for decision making, assuming that other higher level attributes of the distribution are of lesser impact in practical situations. If we use the coefficient of variation as a measure of risk, two choices are apparent as a measure of certainty. First we may subtract the coefficient of variation from unity—if a project is 20% risky, then it is logical to consider it 80% certain. Second, the reciprocal of the coefficient of variation is an alternate measure of certainty—communication engineers will recognize the parallel to the rising information content obtainable with increasing signal-to-noise ratios.

The R&D manager will already have noted how management actions can lower the risk associated with development and product costs by taking steps to bring the mean of outcomes closer to the preestimate and by reducing the coefficient of variation. In addition, the risk can be reduced by breaking a project into tasks and separately estimating each in the expectation that pure chance factors will balance at least part of the time.

At this point it should be questioned whether the straightforward application of knowledge of the probability distribution of outcomes should be directly applied to project selection and evaluation. It is tempting to weight the estimates by the past history of bias in preestimates plus some arbitrary factor times the coefficient of variation and use the result for modifying the costs and benefits in the procedures of the previous chapter. To do so, however, ignores both the role of the product and R&D managers as codirectors of a diversified portfolio of projects and the risk preference function of management.

RISK VERSUS THE HURDLE RATE

Because R&D has the characteristics of an investment, it is appropriate to consider a group of R&D projects in the same terms as a portfolio of tangible investments (Van Horne, 1974). Unless all projects are positively correlated, the level of relative risk of the project portfolio should be lessened by the diversification of projects, just as it is in a stock or bond portfolio.

Following this line of reasoning, a large number of projects should entail a lower risk than a smaller number of projects for the same total R&D budget. Project cost relative to the total R&D budget has been cited as a risk indicator (Schwartz and Vertinsky, 1977).

If we move from R&D manager's viewpoint back to that of the general manager and his financial officer, an even larger portfolio of investments comes into view, including capital projects and market development for extending the business, and the existing business, which is riskier than a riskless investment (say, U.S. Treasury bills). In portfolio theory, there is a systematic relationship between the riskiness of a portfolio and its value in the market—that is, unless a risky investment has a higher return to compensate for the risk, the market will reduce its value to compensate. We may consider this in equation form as follows where risks are positively correlated (shown graphically in Figure 6.2):

$$i = i_0 + a_1\frac{\sigma_1}{\bar{x}_1} + \ldots \ldots a_n\frac{\sigma_n}{\bar{x}_n} \qquad (1)$$

where i = return needed on the portfolio
i_0 = return on a riskless investment

σ_n = standard deviation of the nth group products
$\bar{x}_n$ = mean of the nth group of projects
a_n = weighting factor for the nth group of projects

In the typical business, we can assume the first group of projects maintains the existing business, the next are capital projects, the next promote market development, and so on. Within R&D, projects may be grouped by technical risk and by market (commercial) risk levels.

In portfolio theory, the above worst-case formula is greatly modified according to the covariance of one project with another, reflecting diversification. The formulae get more complicated and will

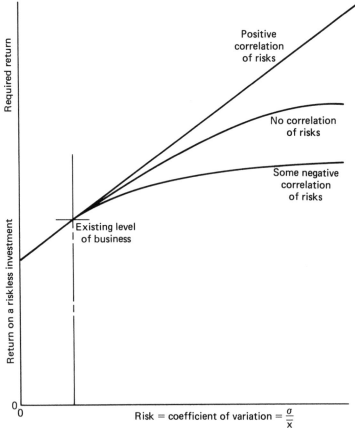

Figure 6.2. Required return versus risk

not be repeated here but are found in most texts on financial management (Van Horne, 1974, Quirin, 1967). However, it is probable that current R&D projects will have a low covariance with then current capital and market development projects, as each is arrived at at a different point in the R&D/product life cycle. R&D projects can be negatively correlated with each other as shown in the following example:

In a company or division of modest vertical integration, a new technology can yield a component that is marketable separately and that can be incorporated into a higher-level product (or system). If both projects are technically successful, their correlation can be quite negative. Commercial success for the component may drive up its price, squeezing margins for the product. Lack of commercial success for the component, particularly if caused by price competition, may lower product cost and enhance its own commercial success.

It can be shown that when an incremental project is negatively correlated with other existing or contemplated projects, it is desirable in order to reduce the total risk of the firm though its own risk be higher (Quirin, 1967, p. 227). This is the reason for example, for the purchase of insurance whose expected outcome is high if and only if the insured project fails.

What does this mean for the practical application of risk to the assigning of a hurdle rate? It means that the use of a linear form of risk assessment such as Eq. (1) is probably too conservative for the average business situation whose required return is more probably near the no correlation of risk curve in Figure 6.2.

A simple example may serve to illustrate. If the treasury bill return is 10% and the existing business returns 20% on investment, a 10% return premium for risk exists. A project portfolio with double the risk of the present business would require a double-the-return premium or 30% total return for a linear positive risk correlation but only a 14% premium (10% $\times \sqrt{2}$), for a total return needed of 24% for a group of projects with no correlation with the existing business.

In the absence of considering management's risk preferences, it would appear proper for the financial director and the R&D manager to make serious study of the types of risks the business faces in moving on from its existing state and how R&D relates to other forms of investments, so as to establish a reasonable return premium for use as an R&D hurdle rate. Risk preferences must be considered, however, as covered in the next section.

A frequently encountered approach is a weighting factor applied either to a year of cash flow, or to size of project. The Kappa Division (depicted in Figure 5.3) calculated payback only after discounting all cash flows (in and out) at a 20% annual rate. Naturally enough, had the payback then been converted to its return equivalent, the indicated return would have been low by about the 20% discounting. Arbitrary coefficients applied to future years achieve the same effect, but are less objective.

Weighting factors applied to the size of the project are derived from considering risk increasing as diversification is lessened (Lindsay and Sametz, 1963). Thus, they are the same type of approach to risk as described earlier in the relationship of project cost to the total R&D budget. Although it may be possible to derive some method of quantifying these factors, any such scheme will be difficult to separate from the subjective judgments related to management's risk preference functions.

The full portfolio theory approach is perhaps too sophisticated for the ordinary mid-sized industrial division or company. Thus, an approach based on increasing the hurdle rate for risk seems an ac-

---

The general manager of the Tau Controls Company reasoned in the 1970s that the principal risk to the benefits side of the decision equation was the lack of certainty of product cost. He tended, therefore, to wait until the end of the feasibility study to begin hard questioning of business feasibility. At that point, he required a 25% adder to product costs in volume production as part of the business analysis. According to the sales-to-cost ratios and investment-to-sales ratios of Tau Controls, the general manager's requirement was the equivalent of a 15% premium on the pretax hurdle rate. When development had produced a working model that could be reviewed by the shop superintendent for reasonability of estimates of time and materials, the general manager lowered the required adder to 15%, equivalent to a 9% hurdle rate premium. Only when development had completed production drawings and these had been costed by accounting with the help of industrial engineering did he consider development risk had ended—a 5% premium was kept, however, to account for manufacturing risks. Since these cost estimates were for volume production, separate additional allowances were made for inefficiencies in manufacturing start-up.

ceptable middle ground, capable of some objective calculation. The principal battle to be faced by the R&D manager is how much of a premium and for which factors. Project size, product extension, new products for existing markets, new products for new markets, commonality of technology with present base, and probability of technical success are all factors affecting technical risk which have previously been mentioned.

One additional factor is increasing certainty during the development period, shown graphically in Figure 4.2. This affects both development cost to complete, and product cost, which affects future benefits. One problem with applying a changing factor for risk-to-development costs is that only after most of the money is spent does the certainty become high enough to be worth lowering the risk factor on a small remainder. Product cost may be a different matter, as shown in the example on the previous page.

RISK PREFERENCE FUNCTIONS

Many people gamble, which implies that they can tolerate risk. Few people, however, gamble with large sums, indicating an aversion to serious risk. The same is true with investors in businesses. Although individual entrepreneurs are risk seeking, they seldom have much of their own capital at the start of a new company. And while venture capitalists are risk seeking, they tend to run very large portfolios as a means of risk limitation. Lage corporations tend to be risk averse since even though stockholders have limited liability, they expect profits and are disturbed by losses.

Economists have spent years studying this phenomenon and deriving theories of the utility of investments under risk. The R&D manager does not have to understand this theory, but only to expect some factor in decision approval equations that represents his management's preferences—usually risk averse, occasionally risk seeking.

If we were to take Eq. (1) and modify it with some additional arbitrary factor to increase risk, the increment could be analyzed by a Taylor series, given the usual mathematical constraints. Since we tend to be dealing with small numbers in coefficients of variation, limitation of the series to its quadratic form seems reasonable as a first approximation. We then express the required return (i) as follows:

$$i = i_0 + \sum_1^n a_n \frac{\sigma_n}{\bar{x}_n} + b \left(\frac{\sigma_p}{\bar{x}_p}\right)^2 \tag{2}$$

where $\dfrac{\sigma_p}{\bar{x}_p}$ = coefficient of variation of the portfolio

b = weighting factor

and all other factors are the same as for Eq. (1). With a plus sign the management is risk averse, and with a minus sign it is risk seeking. Instead of the coefficient of variation of the portfolio, that of individual projects or groups of projects could have been used with appropriate summation.

A principal conclusion of this superficial excursion into the mathematics of utility theory is that risk aversion and the benefits of portfolio diversification have quadratic forms of opposite sign. This is not to say they will exactly cancel in all instances. However, the manager of a small R&D department may take the linear form of Eq. (1) which the author earlier labeled conservative and use it as an uncomplicated working approach explaining to management that it is basically a risk-averse approach to defining a required hurdle rate.

In Table 6.1, derived from Table 5.2 and a generous application of hindsight, Kappa Division's 1976 program in reconstituted to illustrate how a risk assessment might have gone. The estimates had been made by four different section leaders, and the coefficients of variation were determined by looking back at past projects as well as those in the table after completion. The wide spread of coefficients is due less to the capabilities of the section heads than to the level of certainty of the tasks assigned to them—the project leader for the first and ninth tasks was assigned low-certainty projects, and the section head for the sixth and eleventh projects handlled routine tasks along with sales order specials not included in the table. The coefficients are for technical risk only.

The risk aversion is derived also in retrospect by the square of the coefficient of variation multiplied by a weighting factor of 0.0035, which was determined by correlating a number of admittedly subjective judgments made at budget reviews and project approval sessions. Ideally, this risk aversion factor should have been determined beforehand by negotiation with the general manager and the financial director. However, life was all so simple then, and quantification of risk had not yet come to the Kappa Division.

Table 6.1.   Kappa Division Projects with Risk Assessment

Project nos.	Development cost ($000)	IRR (%)	Coefficient of variation (%)	Risk aversion (%)	Corrected IRR (%)
1	956	19.0	34	4.0	15.0
2	505	19.0	27	2.6	16.4
3	398	22.5	15	0.8	21.7
4	51	25.5	15	0.8	24.7
5	48	36.0	15	0.8	35.2
6	46	25.0	10	0.4	24.6
7	490	33.2	27	2.6	30.6
8	210	30.0	27	2.6	27.4
9	145	33.5	34	4.0	29.5
10	98	40.0	15	0.8	39.2
11	105	73.0	10	0.4	72.6

Source.   Table 5.2 plus calculations by author.

The weighted average coefficient of variation was 23.7%. Assuming zero correlation between section heads, but positive correlation of projects under each section head, corresponding to the derivation of coefficients of variation, the weighted portfolio coefficient of variation was 16.5%. In 1976, the parent company objective for the existing business was a 17% premium over a riskless investment for a 15% coefficient of variation of the existing business. Thus, a linear hurdle premium rate was 26.9%, and a portfolio-based hurdle rate premium should have been 18.7% or 8.2% lower. With riskless investments then at 6%, the linear-based hurdle rate should have been 32.9% versus the 30% then used, and on a portfolio basis 24.7%. Looked at on this basis, two of the projects previously rejected moved just to an acceptance level, after a consideration of the preference for risk avoidance and the lower hurdle rate justifiable for a diversified portfolio of projects.

Where an analysis such as this becomes a vital component of the decision, all risks must be taken into account, including the commercial risks ignored in Table 6.1. Thus, departure from a simple linear approach ignoring the partially offsetting risk aversion and portfolio effects is important only when either management's risk aversion is extreme, or a single project or two dominate the R&D budget and thus tend to negate the portfolio effect. Otherwise, the straight line (the higher the risk, the higher the return) is clearly the first-order effect to be taken into account by research managers.

RESEARCH INVESTMENTS UNDER RISK

Thus far, the discussion has been largely about risk as viewed from and potentially measured by the research manager concerned with his department. For a full investment decision under risk, a larger number of risks enter the calculations than are under the research manager's purview. In the author's experience, only the most recent business school graduates in marketing and product management can be expected to employ a method of anayzing risk based on the coefficient of variation. What is possible, however, is to get others to use a decision tree type of quantitative evaluation of the relative levels of risk, as in the following example:

The product manager will usually stand by his estimate, but allow about a 60% confidence factor. The alternatives can be: The product does better than expected (10%); the market did not accept it as well as forecast (20%); there were many problems in moving it (10%). An expectation table of these alternatives folows:

Forecast	Percent	Sales value $	Weighted value
Optimistic	10	120,000	12,000
Main estimate	60	100,000	60,000
Soft	20	80,000	16,000
Dud	10	50,000	5,000
Most probable outcome (total)			93,000

Thus, in this example the risk-weighted outcome for product success is 7% below the main estimate.

The marketing manager may have a similar scale for general market conditions, such as boom 10%, main estimate 70%, soft 15%, recession 5%. This type of assessment for market risk may further reduce the risk-weighted probable outcome.

Decision trees are easy to use, and the shift down of the mean under the typical skewed distributions involved is a reasonable surrogate for risk (although much smaller than the 19% coefficient of variation of the above example). Decision trees have the advantage of taking little of the time of the commercial people whose input is desired, of being readily understood, and of still giving a reasonably quantitative answer to a general manager's question of what is the commercial risk of this project? Like most simple approaches, there has been much theoretical extension of the decision tree approach, including the introduction of utility theory, but the extent of its use in business has not been particularly visible to this author. Further discussion may be found in other texts (Gibson, 1981, pp. 315–320; Quirin, 1967, pp. 206–210).

Another multiattribute approach used to combine financial factors with technical and commercial risks has recently been proposed (Schwartz and Vertinsky, 1977). The financial factors are:

Internal rate of return
Payback period

The discussion in Chapter 5 showed that these measures are interrelated and only the IRR is needed.

The technical risk factors proposed in this multiattribute method are as follows:

R&D cost as a proportion of R&D budget
Probability of technical success
Availability of government funding

The first of these has been noted earlier in this chapter as a valid measure of the risk of nondiversification. The second is a measure of certainty and thus an inverse measure of risk. Government funding is an apparent inverse measure of risk, as the more that is funded by government, the less needs to be funded by the firm. It is only available, however, in certain areas of R&D, and even in these needs to be viewed under the principle of TINSTAAFL (there is no such thng as a free lunch). Far be it from this author to counsel any R&D manager not to line up for available funds from government. However, a financially astute R&D manager will also consider opportunity cost—what is the net present value to the firm of the next project foregone while the engineers are working on a government-funded activity? (Dohrmann, 1982).

The commercial risk factors in the multiattribute approach are as follows:

Probability of commercial success
Potential market share

Probability of commercial success is an inverse indicator of risk, like technical certainty. Potential market share seems to duplicate commercial success probability.

The multiattribute approach suffers not only from the lack of independence of its various factors, but also from the way the original authors and subsequent ones pass through subjective weighing in their attempts at project evaluation (Gibson, 1981, pp. 320–326). Nonetheless, the multiattribute method does produce quantitive weighing of return, technical risk, and commercial risk.

Still another approach is a scoring method based on the product of the probabilities of technical success and commercial success (Merrifield, 1978, 1981). Into commercial success are built both risk and return factors separated into two groups:

1. Business attractiveness
    Sales/profit potential
    Growth rate
    Competition
    Risk distribution
    Industry restructuring opportunity
    Special factors (political, etc.)
2. Company strengths
    Capital requirements
    Marketing capabilities
    Technology base
    Raw material availability
    Management skills

Some of the commercial success factors seem to be technical ones; only 3 out of 12 are factors that affect return, which seems to overweight risk factors; and all of the factors seem to be susceptible to subjective weighting. Many other specifics in factor definition raise questions in this type of methodology.

What has been presented thus far is a continuum from calculation that includes technical risk to cruder probablistic weighing in a decision tree to scoring methodologies involving various degrees of subjectivity (the latter two approaches). Objectivity through calculation is a goal to be pursued. Yet goals must be attainable. Even with subjective inputs, it is better in the author's opinion to score them than to rank order completely subjectively. Most essential in research investments under risk is that both technical and commercial risk factors ae included, but not in disproportion to return.

NONPROBABILISTIC UNCERTAINTY

Thus far it has been assumed that an adequate methodology for project selection and evaluation can be developed based on the first two moments of the probability distribution: mean and standard deviation. With experience indicating that at least the third moment (skewness) needs to be considered in some instances, there is a range of lack of project certainty which cannot realistically be handled by the approaches covered so far in this chapter.

At the outset, it was indicated that uncertainty is defined as a situation in which the probability distribution of outcomes is unknown. For practical reasons this definition is incomplete without

---

Rho Instruments Limited set out in 1975 with an instrument product family development budgeted at $900,000 (all subsequent dollar amounts are in 1975 dollars to remove the high inflation impact of the era). The project was based on 8-bit microprocessors, though Rho's previous experience had only been with 4-bit devices. This should have (but did not) raise a risk flag to management. Another major project with lower technical risk but much higher commercial risk diverted management's attention and some resources.

By 1977, the initial increment of budget had been spent; the project had slipped 1 year, and $600,000 more was estimated for completion. A newly arrived R&D manager recommended termination, but was overruled by the general manager on the subjective advice of product and marketing managment. A new project manager was installed. Six months later, he and a number of the engineers on the project resigned. A third project manager (appointed temporarily) took over for another 6 months until a permanent project manager was hired. A further 18 months was required to finally complete the project at a total cost of $2.2 million.

The present value of the project's potential total sales stayed at $8 million (in constant dollars), so that at each reassessment point, the then visible future outlay (treating all past outlays as sunk costs) appeared large enough to justify continuing the project. Worst-case conditions never entered continuation discussions.

---

the addition of those situations where the probability distribution is excessively skewed. These are the projects that escape R&D management control, or threaten to do so. When faced with them, the R&D manager is less interested in developing or applying a mathematical theory than in obtaining a means of bringing a deteriorating situation under control. The three standard deviation limit provides a workable cutoff point for separating probabilistic inadvertence from impending disaster.

Various game theorists have evolved rules for handling such situations. The only one so far found practical by the author is the "minimax" rule: minimize the maximum regret of possible courses of action. One of these courses of action should be to terminate the project if it exceeds, or threatens to exceed, the three standard deviation limit. A second logical course of action is to continue the project (as in the example) expecting the return from success to recover outlays that are newly incurred, if not those that have gone before.

What characterizes a minimax philosophy is the selection of other courses of action. One of these might logically be to ask, What if the new estimate to complete is proportionally as bad as the first one? Applying this to Rho's case, we find the second estimate was 67% above the first, for a total of $1.5 million. A good "what if" of this type might have added another 67% and asked, What is the regret if the project goes to $2.5 million?

Table 6.2 shows Rho's regret analysis from the first decision point (1977) ignoring sunk costs. Contribution is return before interest and income taxes, after an allowance is made for selling, administrative, and general expenses. Under the minimax rule, the project should have been terminated to avoid the maximum regret of the worst case. Had the contribution forecast been $400,000 or more higher, the maximum regret would have been to terminate, and the project should have been continued. As it actually turned out, the decision to continue does not look so bad until one considers the opportunity cost of that additional $1,300,000 expenditure of R&D. A clear opportunity could have been treated as still another possible course of action—in the emotion of a number of such deteriorating R&D projects, the author has yet to see it so done.

True uncertainty also includes cases where project outcomes are not based on random variables, but rather are subject to the actions of those with the market power to make major swings occur that can have a negative impact. A recent example was the tenfold rise

Table 6.2.   Rho Instruments Regret Analysis

Course of Action	Added R&D costs ($000)	Contribution ($000)	Regret (Profit) ($000)
Terminate	0	0	0
Continue as forecast	600	1,200	(600)
Worst case	1,600	1,200	400
Actual	1,300	1,200	100

Source. Compiled by author from proprietary data.

in crude oil prices organized in the 1970s by the Organization of Petroleum Exporting Countries. A worst-case analysis could have looked at the vulnerability of many projects, however difficult to quantify, to a sudden price rise or lack of availability of a critical material. In the electronics field, sole-source components are a source of uncertainty, and a few sourced ones are risks, with corresponding effects on project selection and evaluation procedures.

Finally, if no other methodology prevails that is acceptable to management, subjective ranking by a number of people (such as a new product selection committee) is an approach to consider. The assets of such a group are a greater total weight of experience than one individual alone could have and an opportunity for conflicting opinions to be mediated or negotiated (Ellis, 1983).

SUMMARY AND CONCLUSION

Project selection and evaluation methodology needs to be modified to reflect risk and uncertainty. Where the number of projects is sufficient, the causes of differing outcomes reasonably random, and the degree of skewness not extreme, probabilistic methods may be applied. Both technical and commercial risks need to be considered with a premium proportional to risks being added to required return as a primary factor in project selection and evaluation. Corporate risk reflecting a portfolio of individual projects tends to lower the required rate of return, but this is often offset by management's tendency to be risk averse. Calculation of probable risks is a preferred approach to scoring methods that involve some subjectivity.

In cases of nonprobabilistic outcomes and high degrees of skewness, minimizing the maximum regret of courses of outcomes is a method for handling uncertainty.

REFERENCES

Block, Robert G., "Ten Commandments for New Product Development," *Industrial Research/Development*, March 1979, 97–100.

Brooks, John, *Telephone—The First Hundred Years*, New York: Harper & Row, 1976.

Dohrmann, R. J., "Quantifying Contract Research Projects," *Research Management*, **25** (2): 30–33 (1982).

Ellis, Lynn W., "The Temporary Group: An Alternative Form of Matrix Management," *Matrix Management Systems Handbook*, ed. David I. Cleland, New York: Van Nostrand Reinhold, 1983.

Gibson, John E., *Managing Research and Development*, New York: Wiley, 1981.

Lindsay, R., and A. W. Sametz, *Financial Management: An Analytical Approach*, Homewood, IL: Irwin, 1963, 56–59.

Markowitz, H., *Portfolio Selection*, New York: Wiley, 1959.

Merrifield, D. Bruce, "How to Select Successful R&D Projects," *Management Review*, December 1978, 25–39.

Merrifield, D. Bruce, "Selecting Projects for Commercial Success," *Research Management*, **24** (6): 13–18 (1981).

Perrakis, Stylianos, and Izzet Sahin, "On Risky Investments with Random Timing of Cash Returns and Fixed Planning Horizon," *Management Science*, **22** (7); 799–809 (1976).

Quirin, G. David, *The Capital Expenditure Decision*, Homewood, IL: Irwin, 1967.

Schwartz, S.L. and I. Vertinsky, "Multi-Attribute Investment Decision: A Study of R&D Project Selection," *Management Science*, **24** (3): 284–301 (1977).

Van Horne, James C., *Financial Management and Policy*, Englewood Cliffs, NJ: Prentice-Hall, 1974.

Wood, Edward C., *Case Studies on the Process of Technological Innovations in the Economy's Private Sector*, Menlo Park, CA: Stanford Research Institute, 1975.

7

MEASUREMENT AND CONTROL

Planning, organizing, measuring, and controlling have been described in countless management books as the continuing work activities of any manager. The first six chapters set the stage for what an R&D manager must do to plan and organize for the economic task of the firm and of the R&D department. His work has continuously been been expressed in terms of the common financial denominator, money. But because a manager primarily manages people, *time applied* is a normal intermediate measure, an acceptable stand-in for financial calculations.

The R&D manager lives within the structure of the operation's finances. Not surprisingly, therefore, he must organize on a budget basis to measure applied time, overheads, expenses, and variances from budget, and to forecast to the end of the budget period in these terms.

The other vital sets of measurements are on a project basis, both for development cost and product cost. Performance must be measured against estimate to obtain the mean and standard deviations of outcomes. The results are used to assess risk and uncertainty in categories likely to be important to future decisions, such as technology, products, and markets, but also by managers and R&D teams to measure the effects of individual people. The measurements must track the progress of the project and allow for feedback to improve performance and for forecasting from progress toward targets to prospective project outcomes.

Measurements set the stage for control, which consists of minimizing deviations from objectives. Objectives are derived from preestimates, often modified to reflect improvements based on learning from past mistakes or on actions taken to improve productivity. Controls may range from simple ones aimed at first-level supervision to the sophisticated techniques needed for major projects involving many engineers.

MEASURING IN BUDGET TERMS

An assumption is made that all budget items have been established along the lines of Chapter 3. The principal categories for which measurements are made are overhead personnel; applied-time personnel; directly charged items, expense items, and allocated items.

Overhead personnel, including the R&D manager, are basically charge from payroll records. If they are on the payroll for the reporting period, their costs should appear in actual overheads. The comptroller should compare the actual and reported costs and compute the difference, or *variance* as it is called in accounting terminology. (Note that accounting *variance* and *analysis of variance* are distinct from the same terms used in statistics.) These costs are controlled by hiring and termination decisions and by properly planning for annual salary increases in both amount and timing.

The same measurement and control of the spread betweeen salary costs and estimates are required for applied time personnel. Measurement and control are also needed for actual and estimated unapplied time. The R&D manager should make sure accounting provides separate reporting on both, with the applied-time actuals and variances computed at the standard overhead rate so they can readily be cross-checked against time records. Verification of the accuracy of time reporting should be done at the first level of supervision to ensure that the input to accounting clearly reflects the separation between time charged (applied) to projects and time charged to overhead accounts, in a manner following the same rules used in budget preparation.

The basic reason for following the above convention is so that separate measurements are kept for spending and level of activity, or *volume,* as it is usually called by accounting to reflect its derivation from manufacturing. The decision to send an applied-time individual for unapplied activities such as training will cause a volume variance which needs to be kept separate for measurement and control from variances due to personnel actions (hiring, termination, etc.).

Although the R&D manager will usually be able to obtain the financial director's agreement to the above approach to personnel accounting, he may find it more difficult to apply measurement and control its materials and other direct charges. At least half of the factories with which the author has come in contact find it difficult to keep material charges by project number in their R&D accounts because they are modeled after administrative accounts where analogous items such as office supplies are charged as overheads. The decision on how much precision in directly charged items is requested has to be tempered by the overall cost to the firm of recording such costs.

Where items are expensed, they appear against overhead budget allocations as actual costs and calculated variances. Control through expense measurements often involves chasing down the original invoices in accounts payable to identify the causes of totals reported by accounting.

Variances in allocated items, which are usually charged to the R&D department at the budget rate, are not within the R&D manager's control, and the ideal of simplicity in management suggests not cluttering up R&D reporting with their fluctuations.

Measuring in budget terms then becomes measuring spending in all accounts for comparison with preestimates at budget time and for measurement of applied time on a departmental basis. Comparisons can then be made with the forecasts of the levels to be charged to individual projects. These straightforward concepts lead to simple controls for examining variances highlighted by accounting and for taking the indicated actions to return more closely to budget levels.

MEASURING IN PROJECT TERMS

Measuring in project terms involves the distinct activities of measuring past performance, measuring current performance, arranging feedback of current performance to first-level supervision, and forecasting probable outcomes based on this feedback.

Measurement of Past Performance

The old aphorisms "what is past is prologue" and "history repeats itself" tend to apply to many R&D organizations. Engineers and scientists are quite resistant to change, and there is much inertia in all but the newest fast-changing technology organizations. It is fortunate for the R&D manager that this is true because it means that measurements of past performance can assist in predicting the future.

Performance in this case is the actual results compared with objectives or preestimates. It does not take into account the correctness of the objectives, only how well they were achieved. For every past full project or separately structured task, it should be possible to extract a series of measurements of actual development cost versus the objective, development cost as a fraction of R&D budget, actual product cost versus the objective, and time elapsed to completion versus the objective.

Other factors that enter past performance can also be identified.

Typically, the estimates are made by senior engineers or first-level supervisors such as section heads. Measuring separately by individuals responsible for estimates is not only necessary for the R&D manager but also very desirable for the individual estimator as the only way for him to know his past biases and fluctuations and where he stands relative to his peers. Other personnel factors found to be significant are team structure, group size, and productive individual positioning (Scott and Simmons, 1975).

Other significant factors are technology, products, and markets. The current state of the art and the position of the project with respect to it may be important in determining where deviations from estimates have occurred or may occur later (Dodson, 1977). An important aspect of the general area of technology is the learning or experience curve in manufacturing (Hein, 1967, Chapter 8). Product classification, which may also turn out to be a significant factor, may be traced in multiproduct firms by the coding system used in marketing for segregation of incoming orders. Market or industry sectors may also affect project outcomes because some industry sectors have more stringent specifications than others, which increases technical and/ or commercial risk.

With a sufficiently large sample, modern techniques of statistical inference are available to determine in a quantitive manner which factors are significant. The first problem of this line of attack is the limited data base encountered by most R&D managers. A second problem is that most such methods are of the "null hypothesis" type and only indicate highly statistically significant factors, not ones that may be significant in a management sense but ones that are buried in the noise of random fluctuations. Also the R&D manager has to identify correctly the possible factors—the statistical methods will only tell that chance plus other unidentified factors account for a part of the incomplete correlation. The R&D manager must decide whether the elegance of these methods is justified, considering the cost of using them and the quality of the data base that can be assembled. Usually the answer is *yes,* but on a limited scale.

Since the R&D manager operates through a level of supervision (e.g., section heads), perhaps the most important management measurement is the mean and standard deviation of past outcomes of development and product cost for his subordinates expressed as a percentage of expected outcome (objective or preestimate). The development cost measurement is a measure of both technical personnel risk and pure technical risk filtered by the supervisor as a communications channel with some characteristic distortion. One or two additional technical risk factors may be worth identifying, but beyond that point, the additional effort probably is not justified by the refinement in accuracy.

The R&D departments' principal contribution to commercial risk assessment is the mean and standard deviations of past outcomes of product cost estimates. Beyond that point, it would appear prudent for the R&D manager to leave commercial risk evaluation to product and marketing management.

Measurement of Current Performance

The R&D manager has only a few means of measuring current performance. Time applied to a project is available from supervisors' records at the timesheet turn-in interval—usually weekly or monthly. Time applied is a useful surrogate for personnel costs, which are reported with some delay by accounting. Thus, if some major deviation from plan occurs, the first-level supervisor should highlight it for R&D management long before the comptroller red flags it for the general manager.

The R&D manager should, however, resist setting up an elaborate scheme to monitor time records. It costs money and duplicates what accounting must do anyway. Since 80% of the variances usually result from 20% of the tasks, a rule for reporting exceptions usually works quite well. Thus, supervisors should be asked only to advise when a project has gone above or below a fixed amount from estimate in a reporting period.

To the extent that other costs are directly charged, it is possible they can be monitored on a project basis with the normal delay through accounting. Otherwise, measuring in budget terms may be the only viable option open.

The third measurement of current performance is progress measured against milestones. Some purists will say that elapsed time is not a proper yardstick of financial performance, which may be strictly true, but there is a high probability that a late project has not had proportionally fewer people working on it. Thus, a high correlation usually exists between cost overruns and time overruns. (Brockhoff, 1982).

One reference gives an interesting picture of performance measured by elapsed time (Sandretto, 1968, p. 175). Forty-four projects in a company characterized by "good engineering peformance" had a mean overrun in time of 13% (standard deviation 15.4%), with a range from 15.4% under to 50% over.

The style in which measurements are presented is an important factor in how readily they can be comprehended. Certainly, the absolute values are needed for accounting and for sophisticated control schemes covered later in this chapter. However, reporting in terms of ratios of performance to estimate conveys more in terms of management problems. Consider for example a report that "project A is at 130% of projected applied time for the third month in a row, and is still slipping schedule." The implications are much more readily obvious than had absolute values been used.

Feedback of Current Performance

The human being is, among other things, a remarkably efficient adaptive control device. As is true with passive control devices, however, humans experience reduced efficiency of control action when there is delay in the feedback path. Since the basic purpose of current performance measurement is control, prompt feedback of progress toward objectives is necessary in the interest of efficiency.

The author early in his career had an opportunity to observe engineering departments where costs were not fed back directly because they were considered confidential information. When finally engineers saw full costs of what they had done, the reaction was invariably, "Why didn't you tel me sooner—I wouldn't have done it that way!" Extensive individual self-policing by engineers given prompt and accurate data lowers the amount of supervision needed and thus lowers overhead.

It is not unusual in many engineering organizations to see projects broken into tasks of 6, 8, or 10 weeks. With the typical accounting department cycle based on the general manager's priorities, feedback from accounting may take 4 to 6 weeks from the end of a reporting period. Thus, accounting costs often are too delayed to be as good a feedback as desired for first-level supervision of projects. The promptness of applied time and milestone progress as feedback devices is of increased importance as the task size is reduced.

Forecast from Current Performance

One of the common causes of overruns is looking back at how much has been accomplished, rather than facing realistically how much still has to be done. A calibration of the early tasks of an extended project often indicates much about the final outcome.

If a project has stayed on schedule but has overrun in cost early in a project, it is a reasonable assumption that the same percentage overrun will be seen at the end of a project unless management action is taken. Thus, if the first task of the project is 30% overrun, forecast the whole project at 30% overrun. If the second task comes in at 20% overrun, progress is being made, but weight the two and forecast the project as 25% overrun. There will be some volatility in these early forecasts, but usually by the time a project is one-third complete, some consistent pattern will have developed to give a good indication of the final result.

This is true also of elapsed time. If the progress has not been complete by the milestone, but the costs do not exceed the estimate, the projected time to complete will be in the ratio of the estimate divided by the actual. Thus, if 10 weeks were allowed and after that period of time 80% of the required work were done, it would be reasonable to forecast $10 \times 100/80 = 12.5$ weeks, or a 25% overrun in elapsed time and in cost as well.

It can readily be seen that the cost at completion may be forecast as the product of the two factors discussed in the previous two paragraphs. Thus, if a task has been only 80% completed by a milestone and has run 20% over in cost, it should be forecast as $120/100 \times 100/80$ or 150% of estimate at completion and should be made a target for serious management action.

Forecasting early and often then becomes still another way of using measurements to highlight the work to be done to meet the economic goals of an R&D department.

SETTING TARGET OBJECTIVES

To be useful, objectives must be attainable. Nothing is more disheartening to the individual engineer or scientist than to be set to a task that is beyond the capacity of the team to do in the time allotted. Knowing the high demand for people with engineering skills, the dispirited worker often simply seeks another job.

Yet goals must also be high, or the economic results of the firm will suffer. The R&D manager must thus seek to raise the standards of the R&D organization progressively from the level found in the initial measurements of past performance.

It can be said, based on many years of personal observations, that the most important objective that an R&D manager must instill in the engineering organization is a commitment to milestone dates.

General managers will growl over development cost overruns, but if a product gets into manufacturing and out to the market in time, the company will maintain its competitive position. Product costs that meet estimates usually have the next priority primarily because of their greater relative weight in the return: The cost of sales for the typical industrial product tends to be in the range of 40 to 60% of ex-works price, whereas the mean of all R&D is 2% of sales (*Business Week,* 1982). This is not to say that meeting development cost estimates is unimportant, but when objectives are being set, it needs to be placed in proper perspective with respect to the economic needs of the firm.

Within the frame of higher management's objectives, the R&D manager's first internal objective needs to be to lower technical risk. The closer it can be brought to the risk of current operations, the more R&D will be considered as a desirable investment in the growth of the firm. Lowering technical risk involves bringing the mean of outcomes closer to estimates and reducing the standard deviation of estimates. It does not mean raising the estimates, although this must be done for the incurable optimists among estimators. General management tends to build in enough contingency in project selection decisions so that the R&D manager need not duplicate the effort. Rather, the objective should be to meet, not beat, estimates of time, product cost, and development cost.

A research manager's second internal objective needs to be productivity improvement. Lowering technical risk will make some progress in this regard. However, real productivity improvement means cost savings to handle the same level of activity or cost avoidance for handling a higher level. Since the bulk of R&D costs are people, this means fewer or less-skilled people for a given level of activity. Productivity can come from better training, better methods, or better tools. Tools, such as computer-aided design, cost capital and need to be justified as with any investment proposal. A continual stress on productivity improvements should ensure that estimates regularly decline for the same level tasks.

EFFECTIVENESS OF TIME AND MATERIALS
AS MEASUREMENTS

Although considerable emphasis has been placed in the preceding sections on the use of time and direct charges such as materials as measurements, it must be cautioned that there is no such thing as a typical man-month in an engineering department (Brooks, 1975).

In the first place, the distribution of creativity is very uneven, even among engineers of the same labor classification. Supervisors are also unequal as estimators. A man-month approach ignores individual skills and the mix of skills within a team.

Second, the team's organization and size have their impact (Scott and Simmons, 1975). Although all time applied is considered productive, communication with other team members eats into individual productivity. Large teams lose productivity owing to their communications needs, as do teams with a single individual, whether supervisor or specialist acting as a bottleneck.

For these reasons, team projects should be estimated as group efforts based on the supervisor's knowledge of team capabilities. Only then does past performance of the same team, or at least one with the same key members, give an indication of probable future outcome against which progress may be compared.

Still other factors may be at work as shown in the following example:

A series of projects were studied at a medium-sized manufacturing company overseas (Brockhoff, 1982). One abnormality in historic results was the reaction of estimators to an approval level above which all development project costs were explicitly controlled. For the controlled group, the median overrun in cost was 14% (S.D.* 28%). For projects below the approval limit, however, the mean overrun in cost was 93% (S.D. 49%). No controls were placed on elapsed time where overruns had a mean of 267% (S.D. 58%). Time and cost overruns were closely correlated ($r = 0.75$).

Measurements such as these are clearly not effective indicators of what is happening and are useless for management control. They are merely symptoms of a cultural behavioral problem involving biasing estimates to avoid the control associated with the approval level, insensitivity to the impact of slippages on the balance of the company, and heavy overcommitment. Thus even when controlled projects met development cost estimates, they did not have enough effort applied soon enough to stay on schedule. Control in such a case can only come from a behavioral change in the whole organization, not from measurements.

*S.D. = standard deviation

The use of financial measurements (including applied and elapsed times as surrogates), requires therefore, discipline in the R&D department, and continuity of teams, supervisors, and structure to be effective for control.

SIMPLIFIED CONTROL BY PROJECT LEADER

Obtaining effective control of projects in terms of financial performance and time usually involves the level of the first supervisor—the project leader, section head, and so on. At the first level of supervision there is detailed knowledge of the task to be done and of the people with which to do it. At this level is full knowledge of applied time, elapsed time, and the best early estimates of product cost. It is also a level where a lot of good talent may be wasted if the control scheme is too complicated.

The introduction of word processing equipment to most engineering departments means that a professionally appearing report can be turned out with little effort. In the first place, a basic form can be created and stored to be used as a primary master for all projects. Suggested headings for this master are as follows:

Form title (e.g., Project Status Report)
Project title*
Date
Project number*
Prepared by
Project team*
Progress this month (followed by 15–20 lines of space)
Milestones (names)*
Project cost estimate
    Original target*
    Previous forecast
    Present forecast
    Actual as of
Product cost
    Original target*
    Previous forecast
    Present forecast

For each project, data for certain items (marked by an asterisk) need to be entered only once at the start of work. This creates a secondary master for each project which may also be stored in the word processor. Previous and present forecasts may also be entered in the master and changed as required.

Thus, each month, the mandatory reporting task involves entering the date and some lines of text in "progress this month," and reporting on milestones, changes in forecasts, and actual development costs as supplied by accounting.

Mu Micro Matrix Corporation used such a system on its word processor with a modern version of slip chart reporting of milestones (McChesney, 1980). The milestone section makes up about the lower 60% of its one page project status report as shown for one project in Figure 7.1 at about the project's midpoint (March 1980). Unusual abbreviations shown are BB (bread board), PWB (printed wiring board), and EDR (engineering data release).

About September of 1979, some slips were noted. Prompt management action allowed these to be recovered in the following 4 or 5 months without modifying later milestones.

A start to release of 16 months would have forecast development costs of 160% of the 26 February 1980 actuals, well below the "present forecast." A large direct charge for preparation of the microcomputer mask represented the balance. The forecast included an extension of scope (tooling) of $20,000, only 4% over objective.

The project was in a lot of product cost trouble at the reporting date with models A and B 10 and 18% over target, respectively.

The simplified control form used by Mu Micro Matrix did what was required with minimal reporting cost. It informed management. It flagged slips, which allowed the section head to take self-corrective action. It permitted development cost forecasts in a plausible manner. And it kept the product cost problem visible while the team worked on it.

This type of control has proved quite effective in many sectors of the electronics business, including instruments and controls. The common characteristics are that individual projects are well specified, have defined and stable interfaces, and can be developed by moderate-sized teams. Larger projects need more sophisticated methods unless they can be modularized into smaller projects.

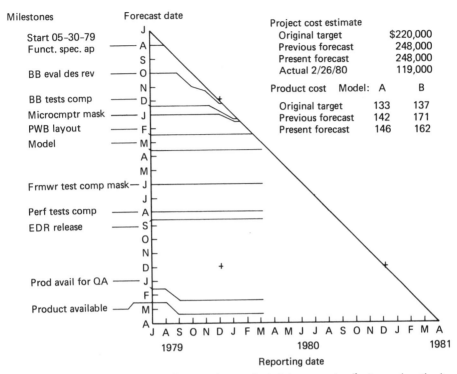

Figure 7.1. Mu Micro Matrix Corporation project status report milestones (portion)

The reader will have noted that this approach to control is derived from the participative/management by objectives school of management. General managers have often asked, Isn't there a more direct way of getting results? Can't you just tell them what to do? Or put in inspectors to keep them in line? This approach goes much deeper when it gets to manufacturing but there the parallel ends. In the factory, even if there is not time to do it right, there is usually time to do it over since production (except for consumer fads) often goes on for years. In development, there is a basic need to do it right the first time or risk missing the market window for the product. Inspection systems fail in development because the costs of policing the many small tasks exceed the benefits obtainable (Brockhoff, 1982). Finally, it costs no more to treat engineers and scientists as adults, and instill in them a sense of self-discipline that takes pride in the success of "on schedule" horizontal lines in a slip chart like Figure 7.1.

COMPLEX PROJECT CONTROL

So much has been written on the subject of the control of complex projects that it is not possible in one section of a chapter to more than summarize some basic principles and give some references for further study. Perhaps the first task is to definee a complex project. It is perhaps easier to define a simple project as one whose team members can be readily controlled by and directly report to a single first-line supervisor and that receives conventional engineering support from central services such as drafting, typing, model making, instruction books, and so forth.

The essence of a complex project is that it requires managing managers or supervisors. Thus, it may require a second level of direct supervision, or may fall into the realm of matrix management (Cleland, 1977 and 1983). Whichever structure is used, it must coordinate two or more first-line supervisors. Based on current costs of R&D, this identifies a complex project as one with an annual spending rate of $500,000 to $1 million or more.

The second element in complex project control is the so called control system. Actually, this system never controls—it is the department or project manager who controls, using the data supplied him from the system. The system based on a plan written when the project is approved, highlights deviations from the plan, but can be no better than the plan as originally prepared. The system goals are meeting the plan technically, economically, and on schedule. Because it must facilitate the control of two or more teams, an element of networking must be built into the system's structure.

As an example, a section of the Mu Micro Matrix Corporation's project described above is shown in Figure 7.2. Activities of a single team are shown as straight lines. The nodes are where two or more teams must have completed their individual tasks before the next activity can commence. This network is representative of the Critical Path Method (CPM) discussed below.

Several widely used complex project control methods may be compared to the desired objectives mentioned earlier. The most widely publicized method is PERT—Program Evaluation and Review Technique—developed by the U.S. Navy in the late 1950s (Sandretto, 1968, Chapter 6; Hein, 1967, Chapter 16; Gray, 1979, pp. 38–40; Gibson, 1981, pp. 282–287). Originally a schedule-oriented system of statistical derivation, PERT called for three time estimates for each activity: best (a), most likely (m), and worst case (b). The best and

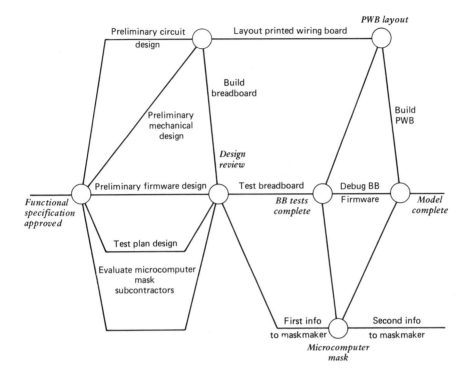

Note: Italicized nodes are reported milestones.

Figure 7.2.   Mu Micro-Matrix Corporation project network (portion)

worst estimates were considered to be three standard deviation conditions, and the outcomes substantially normally distributed. Thus, the mean and standard deviation of the outcomes for each activity were approximated as follows:

$$\text{expected elapsed time } (t_\text{e}) = \frac{a + 4m + b}{6} \qquad (1)$$

$$\sigma_{te} = \frac{b - a}{6} \qquad (2)$$

Based on many years of experience, the author has some problems accepting these equations. Applied to Upsilon Radio's experience cited earlier in this chapter, the PERT standard deviation is about half of their experience. Thus, $(b - m)/3$ would be a closer estimate.

Also, true worst-case estimates are difficult to draw out of supervisors, so it is rare to have a true measure of b.

A later modification of PERT which added the economic factor resulted in PERT-COST (Hein, 1967, pp. 306–308). Each activity was made a sepaate cost segment with a unique charge number. Either t_e or m was used to come to a single cost estimate as the multiplicity of time estimates complicated calculations. The economic difficulty of this method is that it does not provide a good means of forecasting final development costs. The reason is that the costs of actions required to correct deviations from objectives are not reflected in the inputs to cost totals.

Closely related to PERT-COST is CPM, the Critical Path Method (Hein, 1967, Chapter 17; Gibson, 1981, pp. 282–287). CPM uses a single estimate for each activity, versus PERT's three estimates, and thus loses a measure of risk. It does better, however, in developing cost/time tradeoffs and comparing these with market losses or contract penalties to derive meaningful time–cost optima.

Fundamental to CPM is that there is a normal time and cost for an activity handled in an efficient manner and that there is some means of doing the task faster by throwing resources (people, subcontractors, money) at the activity, handling it as a crash program. Thus, direct project (development) costs increase as the project's elapsed time decreases. This direct time/cost tradeoff may be compared with other costs, such as costs as a function of time (e.g., storage, rental of space/equipment), contract penalties (or bonuses), opportunity costs related to time, and so on. Thus, CPM is more sensitive to the economic conditions of project decisions than PERT-COST, and retaining the network structure is also effective for schedule control.

Another method encountered is PACE—Performance and Cost Evaluation (Hein, 1967, Chapter 15). The PACE measurement index is essentially an effect index times an effort rating. The effort index is (number assigned plus loaned less number idle plus absent) divided by (number assigned plus loaned). In other words, it is applied time as a percentage of total time. The effort rating is by nature subjective, but indicates supervisors' views of effectiveness. Five other indices measure personnel as a percentage of plan, budget as a percentage of plan, schedule as a percentage of plan, quality, and shortages. The last three are principally useful in production rather than R&D. PACE type methods are more comfortable for accountants and some general mangers because they treat engineering like manufacturing. The problem with this kind of approach is that it loses end-to-end project focus and lacks the advantage of Critical Path Analysis for focusing on maintaining schedules.

Whichever method of complex project control is chosen, the same needs apply as for simple control. The measurements and their feedback must be prompt. The data must highlight conditions that require management attention to meet the project plan objectives for technical results, elapsed time schedule, and development cost. Simple extrapolation must allow end-of-project forecasting of costs and elapsed time based on progress to date.

SUMMARY AND CONCLUSION

R&D managers must learn to measure progress in the two dimensions of budgets and projects. The firm is budget oriented and measures deviations in spending and applied time. Projects must be measured on the basis of past performance to permit the calculation of risk and to provide guidance for estimating. Current performance must not only be measured, but fed back to development teams with minimal delay and used to forecast critically the potential outcomes of projects.

Objectives need to be set at attainable levels, but at progressively higher goals of reducing the deviations from estimates (technical risk) and improving productivity. So many factors affect time and materials as measurements, they should be used with caution as indicators.

Simplified control needs to track elapsed time (milestones), development cost, and product cost. More complex project control is required when two or more first-level supervisors must be harnessed to common goals. In neither of these cases does the scheme do the controlling; it merely highlights deviations so managers can manage.

It is not difficult for the R&D manager to get so involved in the mechanics of measurement and control that he loses sight of the need to focus primarily on the soundness of business and technical strategies. Achieving tight control over meeting project time and cost objectives will accomplish little if the project does not strengthen the company's competitive position. Measurement and control, therefore, can only be of use if applied to projects that are properly selected and evaluated in the first place.

REFERENCES

Brockhoff, Klaus, "A Heuristic Procedure for Project Inspection to Curb Overruns," *IEEE Transactions on Engineering Management*, **EM-24** (4); 122–128 (1982).

Brooks, Frederick P., *The Mythical Man Month—Essays in Software Engineering*, Reading, MA: Addison-Wesley, 1975.

Business Week, July 5, 1982, 54–74.

Cleland, David I., "Defining a Project Management System," *Project Management Quarterly*, December 1977, 37–40.

Cleland, David I., ed., *Matrix Management Systems Handbook*, New York: Van Nostrand Reinhold, 1983.

Dodson, Edward N., "Technological Change and Cost Analysis of High Technology Systems," *IEEE Transactions on Engineering Management*, **EM-24** (2); 38–45 (1977).

Gibson, John E., *Managing Research and Development*, New York: Wiley, 1981.

Gluck, Frederick W., Richard N. Foster, and John C. Forbes, "Cure for Strategic Malnutrition," *Harvard Business Review*, **54** (6); 154–165 (1976).

Gray, Irwin, *The Engineer in Transition to Management*, New York: IEEE Press, 1979.

Hein, Leonard W., *The Quantitative Approach to Managerial Decisions*, Englewood Cliffs, NJ: Prentice-Hall, 1967.

McChesney, James S., "Project Status Reports—Mo. of March," (Private Communication), April 1980.

Sandretto, Peter C., *The Economic Management of Research and Engineering*, New York: Wiley, 1968.

Scott, Randall F. and Dick B. Simmons, "Predicting Programming Group Productivity—A Communications Model," *IEEE Transactions on Software Engineering*, **SE-1** (4); 411–414 (1975).

8

OPTIMUM RESEARCH AND DEVELOPMENT SPENDING

Every general manager asks the functional department heads to justify proposed levels of expenditure as part of the budgeting process. Resources are never infinite, and all departments would like a greater share of the available funds. The proper amount to devote to R&D can never be zero if the company hopes to have a future, nor can it long exceed the company's pretax income for the same reason. Between these two limits are a fairly broad set of choices for the research manager to propose and justify as a spending level.

HOW MUCH SHOULD A COMPANY SPEND ON R&D?

Answers to the question, How much should a company spend on R&D? have been advanced from the viewpoints of politics, investment theory, item-by-item justification (zero base budgeting), contribution to strategy, and optimization of earnings and of common stock price.

A Political Answer

As a large corporation tends to be a political system, one answer comes from politics: Lobby and fight for as large a budget as you can. Closely allied to this argument is the spend-as-much-as-you-can-afford philosophy (Rosenau, 1980). Stated in such terms, the answer seems tremendously subjective. Over the years, however, the author has seen many silver-tongued colleagues argue this way and have their budgets approved. Sometimes their departments were successful, and sometimes not.

The question of how much can be afforded is often answered by comparison with others in the same industry. This too tends to be subjective since relative efficiencies are not understood as well as other differences between firms.

Some measure of political skill is needed by any research manager. Yet, in the modern quantitative world, a purely political answer to the question of how much should be spent on research and development may not get the research manager much of a hearing.

The Investment Theory Answer

Since research is by its nature an investment, modern investment theory should, in principle, provide an answer. One problem is that there is a bewildering variety of such answers in the literature. The most commonly applied ones are virtual cousins (Quirin, 1967, p. 46):

1. Accept all projects for which the benefit-to-cost ratio is greater than 1.0, using the weighted average cost of capital as a discount rate, or
2. Accept all projects for which the net present value is positive, using the cost of capital as a discount rate, or
3. Accept all projects for which the IRR is greater than the cost of capital.

Naturally, considerations of risk and uncertainty as covered in Chapter 6 may require the appropriate higher hurdle rate. The budget is then the sum of all approved projects, plus assistance as outlined in Chapter 3, plus an allotment of discretionary funds.

There are some difficulties with this approach. First, it requires all projects be approved before the start of the budget year. Particularly in consumer products this may be difficult to do because of short response cycles. Second, it ignores the impact on current earnings of an excessive number of good projects. In a creative R&D department, however, this approach is quite satisfying to the average finance director and other quantitatively oriented members of management.

Item-by-Item Justification

Item-by-item justification has also been advanced as a method of setting a technical budget (Sandretto, 1968). This approach, also known as zero base budgeting, differs from the investment theory approach essentially by assessing the total probable needs of the R&D department, rather than building up a total from approved projects.

The probable scope of new product needs can be determined by a cooperative effort with marketing, using projections from past data to indicate the technical effort required to develop these products. Building a technology or patent position can be similarly estimated. Special manufacturing development can be estimated in cooperation with the manufacturing department. Sales order specials can be estimated with marketing. Engineering support, discretionary funds, and assistance can be added at levels based on past needs. The total will be a "should be" level of R&D effort.

If this approach brings about a total above what can be afforded based on company return goals, some reconciliation becomes necessary. The strength of this approach will depend to some extent on the skill with which it is prepared and presented. In principles, building up from fundamental needs is a sound approach to budgeting.

When the Nu Division of an overseas subsidiary found itself in considerable financial difficulties in the late 1960s, an outsider was hired as division manager to turn things around. The engineering department was quickly reduced from 660 to 405 people. The division manager, unsure of how this would affect the division, called for staff assistance in doing an item-by-item justification of the technical budget.

Of the 405 people, only 135 were found by the staff executive to be working on R&D. Seven layers of supervision were piled up over the development engineers, and this frictional overhead brought with it unneeded supporting staff. After a careful person-by-person analysis, which allowed only two levels of supervision between working engineers and the chief engineer, a department of only 270 people was recommended, including the 135 working on R&D. The division manager accepted the basis for the recommendation and decisively transferred 40 of the surplus people to customer contract engineering and 60 to field contract start-up, both of which were behind schedule. One year later, an assessment of R&D milestones indicated that only between 2 and 5% elapsed time slippage could be attributed to this drastic cutback, principally owing to undersupervision of newer engineers.

As the example illustrates, a careful analysis may show that the R&D budget is too large to be supported by a zero base approach. A manager's people skills may be severely taxed when restructuring to new lower levels of staffing and supervision are carried out.

Contribution to Strategy

As industrial companies get more deeply involved in strategic planning and business development, a new dimension is added to the traditional interface with marketing in the R&D department. Marketing typically thinks in terms of "what our business is and how it should evolve." Business development asks, "What should be our business, should we get there by evolution or acquisition, and what that we are now doing should be harvested to provide funds for this more radical strategy?" To determine a research budget under such conditions, the research manager must have (or acquire) a technical knowledge of opportunities that matches strategic objectives rather than the present business (Gluck, 1976).

The process of establishing an R&D budget under such conditions is a much more fluid one than described earlier. At best, the R&D program may end up refocused at the same spending level, with no wrenching reshuffling of skill mix. At worst, major downgrading may be required in some skill areas, with major new technical capabilities needed in others. In any case, some item-by-item justification will be needed, in association with strategic planning/business development, to establish a suitable R&D spending level.

The Stock-Price Answer

The common-stock-price answer to optimum research spending is cousin to the investment theory answer discussed earlier. Given an efficient stock market, one could expect the price of the stock to reflect all that is known about a company including profits, growth, and the level of R&D spending. Thus, it is reasonable to assume an optimum R&D spending level is one that maximizes the price of a share of the company's common stock.

This approach is a cousin to the investment theory approach because the stock price in an efficient market should reflect the net present value of future streams of income. Thus, the stock price should reflect the choice of R&D projects with positive net present value.

An analysis by Gilman (1978) showed a positive and usually statistically significant correlation between stock-price-to-earnings ratio and research-and-development-to-sales ratio. Although Gilman knew that correlation is not causation, he made the not unlikely behavioral assumption that the R&D-to-sales ratio was the cause. After some manipulation, his study concluded that a company's maximum total-price-to-sales ratio occurs at the optimum level of R&D spending.

The author found difficulty with the direct application of this approach, which includes only an accounting treatment of the effects of R&D on earnings (Ellis, 1980). When applied, this method tends to set too low an optimum R&D level. Attempts to apply this formula to individual product lines produced some conflicting results that a reexamination was made of the formula and its underlying concepts. In many sectors of the electronics industry, levels of R&D spending are comparable with earnings after tax, and it was particularly difficult in these areas to match budgeted levels of spending with calculated optima by the study's formulae.

Simple linear regressions of return-on-sales versus R&D-to-sales ratios gave generally rising levels of earnings with low coefficients of correlation. Since accounting treatment of R&D expense should give declining levels of earnings with increased R&D spending, earnings before research and taxes appeared to be rising at a greater rate than current R&D spending to account for the positive slopes of the regression. Since the levels of R&D-to-sales ratios change slowly with time, this effect is apparently due to the present value of past expenditures discounted by the obsolescence of technology.

Although this study has been found wanting in its method of application, the basic concept is a powerful one which will be addressed again in a subsequent section.

An Earnings Orientation

The division manager to whom the industrial research manager reports is usually rated on earnings performance rather than the price of the stock. Clearly, the research manager needs to understand why an optimum level of R&D spending exists for maximizing earnings and how to determine that level.

The earnings answer to the question, How much should a company spend on research and development? is a direct extension of the optimization problem of microeconomics covered in Chapter 2. It is, however, complicated to the extent that there is a delay in receipt of returns from R&D investment (Parasuraman and Zeren, 1983). Some examples will help to provide the setting for the problem of determining where the optimum is located and what the causative factors are, which differ quantitatively, but not qualitatively, by industry and technology.

The operations-oriented executive may miss the investment nature of R&D, as in the following example:

A new general manager took over the Xi Industrial Products Division about eight years ago where the R&D director had a large, new product introduction program. As each successive product was launched into production, the general manager took the position that that part of the R&D job was done and reduced the technical staff accordingly. For several years the return on sales grew rapidly, both because of the new products and and because of the reduction in expense charged to margins. But then, the competitors' new products began to appear and margins were reduced accordingly to maintain market share. The R&D director with his smaller team was unable to keep up with the competition, and the division fell below the industry norm in profits.

There must of course be an upper limit on the fraction of sales that can be devoted to research and development because the accounting treatment calls for expensing rather than capitalizing these outlays. Another example follows:

Omicron ElectroMechanical Corporation's product line had long product life cycles, a high degree of vertical integration, and good profitability. Nearly 20 years ago the company realized that the semiconductor revolution was going to change its present product line to an electronic one in time, and an appropriate R&D program was started. The R&D director, however, failed to perceive the shorter life cycle of electronic products, and so planned on continual vertical integration. By the time the first product was ready, it was later than competitors' and nearing obsolescence. His response was to request an increased R&D budget to meet the shorter life cycle, while maintaining the traditional approach of a complete product line as requested by marketing and vertical integration as requested by manufacturing, neither of which wanted to change. Several general managers since have followed each other after continued unprofitable years caused by excessive R&D-to-sales ratios.

Intuitively, an optimum level of R&D expense should fall between the extremes of the above cases. A major econometric model based on multiple lines of business gives evidence that an optimum level does exist for maximizing earnings (Strategic Planning Institute, 1977). However, the construction of this multiclient model requires anonymity of inputs, with the result that there is a lack of causative explanation. The dependant variable in this model is operating return (pretax, preinterest) on investment, which is one possible criterion for evaluation.

The Pi Chart Instrument Division attempted to use the stock-price answer to establish the level of R&D spending (Gilman, 1978). It was dissatisfied with the results, but found the approach was modifiable to earnings optimization. Their R&D director realized that return on sales treated in a linear regression with R&D spending for his industry would give him an intercept (ROS at zero R&D) and a slope defining the first two terms of a Taylor series approximation. A third term could be derived from internal accounting data showing that an expenditure of 10% of sales for R&D would wipe out pretax earnings. Thus, for 1977 spending, the following formula was derived from the three sets of boundary conditions:

$$ROS = 2.6 + 0.61R - 0.087R^2 \tag{1}$$

where ROS = return on sales in percent
      R = research-and-development-to-sales ratio in percent

Following the calculus for determining an optimum, this formula gave an R&D-to-sales target of 3.5% and a long-term return result of 3.7% of sales. After consultation with the division manager, R&D was held to 4% of sales in 1978. Other steps were taken within the division to raise margins to meet company objectives.

By mid-1978, industry results had shifted so much that the linear regressions gave a higher ROS intercept with a lower slope. The margins had improved so that now 12% R&D to sales would be required to wipe out pretax profit. A new equation was calculated as follows from the revised boundary equations:

$$ROS = 3.8 + 0.4R - 0.060R^2 \tag{2}$$

where terms are the same as for Eq. (1).

This gave a new optimum R&D of 3.3% of sales and a longer-term prospective ROS of 4.5%.

The example points out several difficulties in using an earnings approach. Industry statistics are somewhat volatile. Many factors besides R&D have their impact on return on sales. There is no guarantee that only a three term Taylor series is a good approximation, although a plausible derivation will be attempted in the following section. The earnings approach says nothing about the quality of the projects nor of their relation to the strategic objectives of the company. Finally, a focus on current earnings ignores the investment theory approach with its balance between current income and growth for maximum net worth of the firm.

This brief review of concepts sets the stage for the derivation of the appropriate quantitative formulas by highlighting the basic causative factors. Some research spending causes an increase in returns by its above-unity benefit-to-cost ratio. The investment nature of R&D creates a multiplying factor based on past research-spending levels, their rate of growth, and the rate of obsolescence of the research work. Diminishing returns and the accounting treatment of R&D ensure that an excess level of R&D spending will penalize current profits. Combining these factors should produce the equation for the optimum spending level for maximizing earnings. Multiplying this equation by the equation for price-to-earnings ratio, an indicator of the level of research spending, should result in an equation for the optimum spending level for maximizing the stock price.

NET EARNINGS AS A FUNCTION OF R&D

A division manager's performance evaluation is usually related to his unit's earnings. Thus, the unit's overall budget presentation may tend to "suboptimize" R&D budget levels according to a perception of their impact on earnings, rather than according to a perception of their impact on earnings, rather than according to the price of the parent unit's stock. Earnings, however, are influenced by many factors other than R&D, such as market share, economies of scale, and so forth. Some managers may not fully appreciate what technology can do for their unit's earning power.

It is particularly useful to study the experience of the electronics industry (computers, instruments, semiconductors, etc.) which dominates the list of businesses with a high ratio of R&D expenses to sales. The semiconductor industry's position at the low end of the list of sales-per-employee ratios gives an indication of relatively low economies of scale, which facilitates intercompany comparisons. Thus, these industrial groups, and particularly the semiconductor companies, should be expected to demonstrate more clearly where an optimal level of R&D budget exists than others with much lower R&D-to-sales ratios.

Fortunately, one after-effect of the adoption of Standard no. 2 of the Financial Accounting Standards Board has been to make available a wealth of essentially comparable information on companies' actual levels of R&D expense (*Business Week*, 1978). In addition, this standard unifies the accounting treatment of R&D as an expense so that any distortions that may once have derived from the capitalization of R&D are now eliminated. The data also show that, in most companies, R&D-to-sales ratios change very slowly from year to year.

If R&D expense had no longer-term "investment" impact, it could be expected that the new accounting treatment would reduce earnings by the after-tax effect of increasing R&D levels. Contrary to this interpretation, simple linear regressions of return-on-sales (ROS) versus R&D-to-sales ratios give generally rising levels of ROS for all sectors of the electronics industry. Correlation coefficients are generally low, which gives an indication of probable additional causative factors. Because of the expense accounting of R&D, earnings before research and taxes must be rising at a still greater rate with increasing research spending to reflect, at rates comparable to those of the current years, the present value of previous R&D expenditures that have not yet become obsolete. As noted earlier, these regressions can only reflect an initial trend because at high R&D-to-sales ratios the expensing of R&D will ultimately be reflected in the bottom line as lower profits.

Of the many different methods of benefit measurement and resource allocation that have been put forward (Baker, 1975), most rank projects by some measure of utility, in the manner shown in Figure 5.6. These measures of utility may be pretax or aftertax in impact, according to the methodology, but must relate in some manner to the prospective net income expected to be derived from the project.

Either the budget level is set first, which establishes a desired cutoff level of utility, or vice versa. The consequence of ranking projects is that the marginal utility of each successive project declines with increasing R&D expense, and the R&D budget is set equal to the sum of all projects with utilities higher than the cutoff point. For a first approximation, a linear slope can be used to desccribe the relative utility of a project according to the following equation:

$$U_n = U_1 - K_1 R \tag{3}$$

where U_n = utility of the nth project
  R = R&D-to-sales ratio
and
  K_1 = a constant

The total utility of any year's R&D budget is composed of the sum of the utilities of all projects above the cutoff level. With the linear approximation cited above, simple geometry will show that the total utility of the budget is the area under the linear slope, which may be expressed by the following equation:

$$b_r = U_1 R - \frac{K_1}{2} R^2 \tag{4}$$

where b_r = the total utility of the current R&D budget
and the other terms are the same as in Eq. (3).

The net utility causing an increase in the current year's earnings before R&D and taxes is the sum of the utility values from prior years' R&D budgets, each depreciated by an obsolescence factor. Because a generally linear relation exists between this increase in earnings and the measure of utility that is used, even after current expenses that do not directly produce current benefits are subtracted, earnings will appear to have a quadratic relationship to the R&D-to-sales ratio. Thus, they will increase with increasing R&D, but finally begin to fall owing to the square of the R&D-to-sales ratio term derived from the declining utility of the lower ranked R&D projects.

Comparing Eq. (4) with Pi Chart Instrument's Eq. (1) and (2) gives a theoretical explanation for the earnings behavior here described. There is a component of return on sales independent of R&D. A linear term positively increasing with R&D spending reflect the utility of the projects of current and prior years. The negative quadratic term represents the diminishing returns of continuing to raise R&D spending in the face of lowering per project utility.

With a slowly growing (or declining) R&D-to-sales ratio, each year's benefits may be modified by a term e^{gt}. The effect of obsolescence may equally be taken into account by a depreciation term $e^{-\delta t}$. This may be then summed by integrating into a total benefit over partial time intervals and relating to resulting earnings in the following equation:

$$\frac{E_{pr}}{S} = K_2 \int_{t_0}^{t} b_r \, e^{-\delta t} \, {}^{g t} e \, dt = \frac{K_2 b_r}{\delta - g} + K_3 \delta > g \qquad (5a)$$

$$= \frac{K_2}{\delta - g} \left[U_1 R - \frac{K_1}{2} R^2 \right] + K_3$$

where E_{pr} = earnings from prior research
  S = sales
  K_2 = constant of proportionality
  K_3 = constant of integration (return on sales with no R&D)
  t = time
  g = growth in R&D budget with time
  δ = depreciation of past R&D time

and the other terms are as defined in Eq. (3)

Equation (5) only applies if the obsolescence rate is greater than the growth rate. Typically obsolescence is at least 20 to 30% per year in the electronics industry so this is probably true for most companies whose R&D growth rates are similar to sales growth, currently 10 to 15% per year.

If we take earnings before research (both prior and current) and taxes as representing the constant term in Eqs. (1) and (2) and assume current research is not yet contributing to current earnings, we may derive the ratio of after tax income to sales (ROS) from the following formula:

$$\text{ROS} = \frac{E_{at}}{S} = (1 - T) \left[\frac{E_{br}}{S} + \left(\frac{K_2 U_1}{\delta - g} - 1 \right) R - \left(\frac{K_1 K_2}{\delta - g} \right) R^2 \right] \qquad (6)$$

where E_{at} = earnings after tax
  T = fractional tax rate, before R & D tax credit.
  E_{br} = earnings before research and taxes
and other others as previously defined.

From Eq. (6) it can be seen that a high initial project utility, a low obsolescence rate, and a high real growth of R&D expense all contribute to a high initial slope for return on sales versus R&D-to-sales ratio. At high R&D spending, the decline in project utility greatly decreases return on sales. By differentiation and regrouping terms, the optimum level of R&D spending (R^*) for maximizing earnings is found to be as follows:

$$R^* = \frac{U_1}{2K_2} + \frac{g - \delta}{2K_1 K_2} \tag{7}$$

The same three factors also contribute in the same sense to a high optimum level of research spending for maximizing earnings. Because the formulas are invalid if $g \geq \delta$ and because obsolescence rates are usually beyond the R&D manager's purview, the factors that can really to be controlled are the utility of the best project and the fall-off rate to the cutoff point (K_1). This conclusion tends to support the investment theory answer to the spending question—find good projects from an investment viewpoint and build your R&D budget around them.

Just as growth raises the optimum R&D spending level reflecting the investment impact of R&D, so a declining R&D-to-sales ratio lowers the optimum level, reflecting disinvestment in the future. This, then, begins to explain the degenerative case given earlier in the example of Xi Industrial Products. The connection is logical because a focus on current earnings is a focus on all but the future exemplified by R&D.

Experience with internal company data has shown that calculations of the optimum R&D level for the purpose of maximizing earnings give reasonable results within individual lines of business, but the effect is quickly obscured in the aggregate of a number of product lines. A similar obscuring effect also appears in much of the published data and is readily apparent in the semiconductor industry, characterized by high technology and low economies of scale, where firm size has a proportionally lower effect on return on sales than in other industries. Twenty-one samples over two years (1977–1978) are shown in Figure 8.1. A quadratic regression of return on sales for this industry versus the R&D-to-sales ratio is shown in this figure

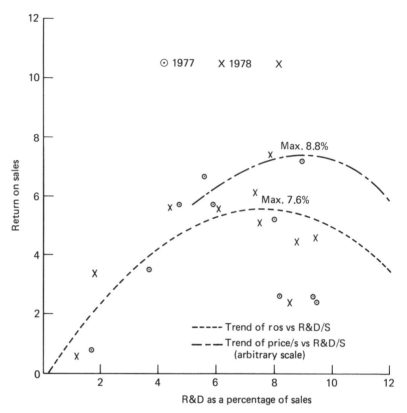

Figure 8.1. Return on Sales versus R&D/Sales for Semiconductor Industry (1977/1978). (From Ellis, 1980. Copyright Research Management.)

as the lower curve. In terms of earnings maximization, the optimum R&D spending for this industry at the time was 7.6% of sales, with a correlation coefficient of 0.51 which is significant at the 1% level.

This optimum level was quite sensitive to the data from the semiconductor industry's most profitable firm. Without it, the optimum level fell to 6.0% of sales, and the correlation coefficient rose to 0.62, highly significant at the 1% level. A look at the data and the regression curve shows, however, that the maximum ROS holds over a broad range of R&D-to-sales ratios. Thus, the company or division manager has wide discretion in selecting a proposed level for R&D budget proposals for management.

PRICE PER SHARE AS A FUNCTION OF R&D

The conditions for maximizing the price of a share of common stock can be derived in terms of maximizing the ratio of the price to the underlying sales per share. This normalized price can then be compared with other companies in an industry without distortion from the differences in numbers of shares outstanding.

The price-to-sales ratio is mathematically the product of the price-to-earnings (P/E) ratio and the earnings-to-sales ratio (ROS), all understood to be on a per share basis.

For most industries, the P/E ratio rises with increasing R&D-to-sales ratios, which reflects the market's appraisal of the "off the balance sheet investment" of R&D conducted in the past, generally at similar R&D-to-sales ratios. This past R&D is expected to contribute to growth and is therefore analogous to the market's evaluation of retained earnings as reflected in the capital assets pricing model (Van Horne, 1974). Although retained earnings are on the books, and past R&D is not, the market reflects the investment nature of R&D and raises the price-to-earnings ratio accordingly. This can be expressed as follows:

$$\frac{P}{S} = \frac{P}{E_{at}} \times \frac{E_{at}}{S} = \frac{E_{at}}{S} \left[\frac{P}{E_0} + K_4 R \right] \qquad (8)$$

where $\left(\dfrac{P}{E}\right)_0$ = the P/E ratio at no R&D spending

P = price of the common stock per share
S = sales per share
E_{at} = earnings after tax share
R = R&D-to-sales ratio
K_4 = a constant of proportionality

When Eq. (8) is expanded by substituting Eq. (6), a cubic equation for the price-to-sales ratio results with an optimum that is different from that determined for maximizing earnings. The analytical treatment of the formula is rather complex and unrevealing and so will not be completed here. Reflection shows, however, that in the useful range of R&D to sales, the maximum of the price-to-sales ratio should occur at a higher level of R&D to sales than was established above for earnings maximization, but not much higher.

For the semiconductor industry, the trend of the P/E ratio to the R&D-to-sales ratio has been calculated as a linear regression, and then combined with the previous ROS to R&D-to-sales calculation. The result is shown on an arbitrary scale as the upper curve in Figure 8.1. The maximum price-to-sales ratio occurs at an R&D-to-sales ratio of 8.8%, giving an optimum R&D budget 16% higher than one based just on maximizing earnings. Over one-half of the company results are clustered with 1.5% of either side of this value of the R&D-to-sales ratio which maximizes the share price and demonstrates that many semiconductor firms tended in 1977–1978 to behave in a price-maximizing manner, although for some, to do so represented levels of R&D expenditures that penalized current earnings.

One caution also comes from considering the expanded version of Eq. (8). Because the equation is cubic, and the cubic term has a negative sign, the rate of fall-off in price with increased research spending beyond the optimum is quite rapid in the model. No examples to confirm this have been found in published data, nor would one expect them to be found since management would naturally be inclined to curtail R&D spending for its short-term positive impact on current earnings before such an excessive level were reached on any major product line.

It should be noted that not all authorities agree with the arguments presented in this chapter (Rosenau, 1980). Points of difference include the effects of accounting, the masking of the impact of R&D by a variety of other factors, random fluctuations, attempts to stabilize staffing levels, which cause effectiveness to vary with time, and the ironic proposition that profitability may cause more R&D spending simply because more money is available to be spent. Despite the possibility that these factors may mask how precisely an optimum is quantified, the modern research manager has an obligation to answer quantitatively the question, How much should be spent on R&D? This model is an attempt to build a foundation for the answer.

SUMMARY AND CONCLUSION

Many authors have proposed answers as to how much a company should spend on R&D. Some argue politically and subjectively for as much as the company can afford or as large a budget as can be fought for successfully. More objective answers derive from investment theory, which calls for approval of all projects that add to the net present value of the firm, and from zero based budgeting or item-by-item justification, which call for construction of a budget based on quantified itemized need. Mechanistic optimization models proposed earlier have been based on maximizing earnings, which tends to short-change future-oriented R&D, and maximizing common-share price which is akin to investment theory. Some elements of more than one approach may serve the research manager's quest for a fair share of the limited resources of the firm.

A more complex but realistic model has been developed to stimulate thinking at all levels of management about the impacts of R&D budget levels on earnings and share prices. Two different optimum levels of R&D investment exist. The lower of these corresponds to the typical division manager's preoccupation with maximizing earnings over the longer term. Maximizing the price of a share of common stock results in a higher level of R&D budget because of the market's interpretation of higher R&D budget levels as analogous to retained earnings, which contribute to growth. The knowledge of these two different optima should be helpful to the industrial research director in determining annual budget proposals and defending them to various levels of higher management.

At higher management levels the quantitative approach cautions against the tendency of not only division managers' budgeting too little R&D so as to enhance current earnings, but also underscores the need to push for higher-than-earnings optimum R&D budgets to build up the company's growth rate. In any case reflection on the investment nature of research and development and the benefits that result from it should be an important factor in the economic planning of research.

EXERCISE

Assume that Gamma Products' industry had a price earnings ratio approximated by 3 + 3 (R/S), where R/S is the R&D-to-sales ratio in percent. Using your answer to Exercise 1 of Chapter 2, calculate for Gamma Products where the stock price is maximized with respect to sales and compare with actual R&D-to-sales ratios. Did Gamma follow an optimum strategy for a publically listed company?

REFERENCES

Baker, Norman, and James Freeland, "Recent Advances in R&D Benefit Measurement and Project Methods," *Management Science,* **21** (10); 1164–1175 (1975).

Business Week, July 3, 1978, 58–77; and annually to July 5, 1982, 54–74.

Ellis, Lynn W., "Optimum Research Spending Reexamined," *Research Management,* **23** (2); 22–24 (1980).

Financial Accounting Standards Board, *Statement of Financial Accounting Standards No. 2—Accounting for Research and Development Costs,* Stamford, CT: October, 1974.

Gilman, John J., "Stock Price and Optimum Research Spending," *Research Management,* **21** (1): 34–36 (1978).

Gluck, Frederick W., Richard N. Foster, and John C. Forbis, "Cure for Strategic Malnutrition," *Harvard Business Review,* **54** (6): 154–165 (1976).

Parasuraman, A., and Linda M. Zeren, "R&D's Relationship with Profits and Sales," *Research Management,* **26** (1): 25–28 (1983).

Quirin, G. David, *The Capital Expenditure Decision,* Homewood, IL: Irwin, 1967.

Rosenau, Milton D., "Problems with Optimizing Research Spending," *Research Management,* **23** (6): 7 (1980).

Sandretto, Peter C., *The Economic Management of Research and Engineering,* New York: Wiley, 1968.

Van Horne, James C., *Financial Management and Policy,* Englewood Cliffs, NJ: Prentice-Hall, 1974.

9

THE BUDGET
RATIONING
PROBLEM

Previous chapters have made the implicit assumption that the quantity and availability of money were not problems, given returns exceeding the cost of obtaining incremental capital. In the real world, however, for reasons internal to the firm or resulting from external circumstances, added capital may be hard to obtain. This chapter analyzes the underlying reasons for constraints on the size of budgets and considers strategies for choosing the best set of projects. Initially, separate independent opportunities are studied in a single time period of restraint to minimize the adverse impact of a budget limitation. This point of view is then expanded to consider, first, initially exclusive opportunities, and, then, projects that span two or more budget periods.

ORIGINS OF THE PROBLEM

Budget rationing is a necessary task of the research manager whenever the research budget is fixed by higher management at a level lower than it would be had it been built up item by item, as described in the previous chapter. The cause of this constraint is higher management's perception that money will be hard to get in the period for which budgets are being prepared, owing to either internal or external reasons.

The internal reasons may lead to a management decision to limit the total availability of investment funds, including R&D expenditure, or to set evaluation criteria more stringent than the weighted cost of capital plus normal risk premiums. The self-imposition of such limits can arise from a number of causes. There may be an extreme risk aversion on the part of a management that is wary of the affect on the company's image in financial markets of assuming an increased debt load. This attitude may show up in annual reports trumpeting, "Our company's debt-to-equity ratio is at a 10 year low at 40%." Another reason, particularly in venture firms, is that insider management may have reasons not to wish to dilute their control by issuing new common stock equity. A third reason, affecting R&D more than other capital investments, is the desire to avoid the impact of long-term investment on current profits. Whereas a part of capital investment does not lower current profits, sales taxes, investment tax credits, first-year depreciation, and all of R&D expense flow down to the pretax bottom line. Whatever may be the cause of internal restraints on R&D spending, the effect is to lower the long-term growth of the firm and usually, therefore, lower the net present value of current plus future income streams.

If a company decides, for internal reasons, to limit the availability of funds for investment, it falls to the general manager to apportion what monies are available between capital and R&D projects. The division may be made on the basis of rational comparison of alternatives or may arbitrarily reflect its anticipated impact on net income or management's risk aversion. Given the final reduced R&D budget, the research manager will wish to evolve a strategy for cutting back or deferring projects with the least future financial impact. That is, he will want to reduce as little as possible the net present value of the program's benefits less its costs.

Increasing the hurdle rate (before risk premium) to above the market rate for new capital is another common rationing tactic used by higher management. When a firm sets a hurdle rate of 30% (pretax, preinterest) even though its cost of capital is only 23%, it is in effect assuming more difficult times ahead and preparing for a future period of tighter money. It can then evaluate all projects on the basis of the question, What if times were bad? This is, in effect, another facet of risk aversion. Again the research manager must react to minimize the impact on the net present value of the R&D program.

Although the latter approach makes a discount rate available for the use of the methods of financial analysis discussed in earlier chapters, it dodges the real question of the opportunity cost of the excess funds. Rarely are returns as high for a business in the open market as in its own industry.

More compelling are external reasons for limiting a company's investment and R&D programs. To understand this it is necessary to return to the subject of marginal analysis (Chapter 2). A substantial portion of funds available for new investment come from internally generated cash flow: retained earnings and depreciation. The weighted cost of capital in this case is the cost of servicing the present common stock and preferred stock equity plus present debt. To expand beyond this limited positive cash flow requires assuming new debt or new equity or a combination of both. In the case of a company that makes frequent trips to the capital markets (e.g., a public utility or AT&T), the marginal cost of capital may not differ greatly from the average cost of capital. For some companies, however, borrowing at the margin is increasingly expensive. Indeed, where bankruptcy is imminent, or feared, issuing new debt or equity may not be possible at all (e.g., Consolidated Edison of New York in the mid 1970s).

It is reasonable, therefore, to expect that as the R&D and capital investments grow, the costs of capital will also grow at the margin. The hurdle rate is then logically set at the marginal cost of capital, instead of the average cost. This is shown graphically in Figure 9.1 where the cost of capital has been added to Figure 5.6. High-return projects will still be accepted, and lesser-return proposals analyzed marginally.

The effect of the R&D tax credit in the Economic Recovery Act of 1981 (described in Chapter 2) is to raise the utility of projects to the right of cutoff in Figure 9.1. Since the firm must raise more money at the margin to fund an increased R&D budget, the hurdle rate for the incremental projects should also rise.

When the marginal borrowing rate is rather higher than the rate at which the firm could invest funds external to the business, more complicated strategies are required (Bierman and Smidt, 1975). It may not be possible to invest all funds available in internal projects at the marginal rate. In this case, rather than invest the surplus externally at a lower rate, some other internal projects may be more desirable. Under these conditions, all projects with a positive net present value at the marginal borrowing rate would be accepted; all projects with a negative net present value at the market lending rate would be rejected; and where the remaining projects fall becomes a matter for internal negotiation between general, financial, and technical management.

It is also possible for nonfinancial external reasons to cause a limit to be placed on the size of the R&D budget. Skilled people for certain projects may not be obtainable if growth is too large or too rapid. Specialized facilities may be in short or delayed supply (e.g., development computers). These deficiencies will in turn further modify the rationed budget. Even so, it should not lead to the acceptance of projects for which the net return at the market (lending) rate is negative. To prevent the financial manager frm investing externally, the research mnager should have a selection of potentially high-return projects in the discretionary area under consideration by those staff members who are currently available.

Whatever the reasons for budget limitations, the research manager is placed in a position opposite to the one he occupied in the previous chapter where budgets were built up logically from a base. Now the submitted budget must be pruned down with the minimum financial damage. This sounds simpler than it often turns out to be, as shown in subsequent sections.

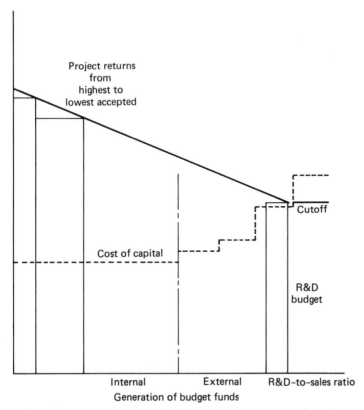

Project returns
from
highest to
lowest accepted

Cutoff

Cost of capital

R&D
budget

Internal   External   R&D-to-sales ratio
Generation of budget funds

Figure 9.1.   Project selection versus marginal cost of capital

MINIMIZING THE COST OF CONSTRAINT

The most straightforward case to analyze is when the constraint applies for only a single time period—usually the upcoming budget year—and the set of projects are separate opportunities without mutual interaction. The problem is to choose the best set of investments for the firm which minimizes the cost of constraint. In practice, this is the situation that faces most R&D managers annually and whose decision-making process extends to and is modified by the more complex situations covered later in this chapter.

A logical manner of handling this rationing is to rank-order projects, as shown graphically in Figure 9.1 and to accept the highest-return projects until the mandated budget level is reached or the hurdle rate is reached, whichever constraint was imposed by management. It is easy to visualize in Figure 9.1 that the firm does not lose very much by eliminating the project "lowest rank accepted" because its return is only slightly higher than the marginal cost of capital. A more severe budget pruning would cut back higher-return projects with lower marginal cost of capital and with increasing loss of future net worth to the firm. Even so, such a procedure preserves the most valuable portion of the R&D program.

As was pointed out in Chapter 5, there are multiple ways to rank projects. The ranking method chosen should be one of *relative* comparison, such as benefit-to-cost ratio (BCR). Although net present value (NPV) is the ultimate ranking method for the portfolio of projects,· a single large project may have the highest NPV, but a low ratio of NPV to cost. Thus, several smaller projects, but with higher BCRs, may yield a higher NPV for the program as pruned.

Using BCR at the hurdle rate gives the most nearly theoretically correct ranking because the hurdle rate should reflect closely the opportunity cost of the next most suitable investment internal to the firm. Internal rate of return (IRR) implicitly assumes reinvestment of funds at the IRR, which does not have a relation to opportunity cost. While the two measures were shown to track reasonably well in Chapter 5, most authors on capital budgeting give examples of where different results can occur depending on the ranking method chosen (Quirin, 1967, Chapter 9).

One of the favorable results of such a ranking approach is that higher-return projects naturally result in shorter cash flow payback, which assists in creating conditions of liquidity that tend to minimize the constraint to a single period. The research manager may be quite uncomfortable with such an approach with its short-term horizon. Marketing may also be uncomfortable since high-return cost reduction and value analysis projects may tend to be favored over new products that replenish the product catalog. Many of these reactions result from considering only a single time period, without considering the impact of deferring projects into a subsequent budget year. Nonfinancial constraints such as deficits or surpluses in certain technical skills tend not to be factored into such a simple, purely objective rationing technique.

Thus far, only the decision processes of a single business unit or R&D department have been considered. As organization size grows, with multiple R&D units, manual methods become more complex to apply. Those readers familiar with computer applications will recognize the rationing problem (as well as the initial budget-setting task) as a classic linear programming problem of the form: Maximize

A, subject to B, C,. . . . Thus the desire is to maximize the net present value of the R&D program, subject to the constraint of budget size or hurdle rate (Weingartner, 1963). Setting up such a linear program in the large organization has in addition the desirable feature of allowing the use of additional constraints such as the skill mix available, the maximum and minimum budget sizes of subunits, multiple periods, and so on (Baker et al., 1976).

MUTUALLY EXCLUSIVE OPPORTUNITIES

Whenever two or more ways exist to handle a project, there is a problem of mutual exclusivity. This problem is complicated in budget rationing when projects involve different scales in value or time. For example, it may be possible to build a dam on a river to any one of three different heights. Building any one excludes the other two. In budget rationing when the highest dam has been chosen but will not fit in the single budget period, a choice must be made to scale down the project, which of course forecloses the full project, or to change the rate of expenditure and delay completion to a later period.

In modern microelectronic-based systems this choice appears frequently because there is an abrupt step between the capabilities, architecture, operating systems, and programming languages of microprocessors. It is not unusual for engineering and marketing, after putting together a project using, say, a 16-bit microprocessor, to find this is one of the lower-ranked projects that must be cut in budget pruning. The choices are: delaying by staying with the initial concept but at a lesser rate of expenditure, or falling back to what could be handled in an 8-bit microprocessor, with lesser costs but also lesser benefits from the exclusion of that part of the market that the 16-bit solution would have captured.

Let us assume that project A (16-bit) has a benefit-to-cost ratio of 1.4 at the original hurdle rate and project B (8-bit) of 1.8. If project A were twice the discounted cost of project B, a fictitious project F equal to the difference between A and B, would have a BCR of 1.0, which is still acceptable at the old hurdle rate. If rationing were done by a higher hurdle rate, the BCRs for A, B, and F might by reduced to 1.1, 1.4. and 0.8, respectively. That is, the fictitious project F shows that the investment in the larger 16-bit microprocessor project A is not a financially desirable activity at the new hurdle rate and that, by financial criteria, the 8-bit microprocessor project should replace it. At this point, the research manager should expect an uproar from marketing and long faces in the technical department staff who are naturally more interested in the more sophisticated project. In the author's personal experience, following the mutually exclusive project approach to budget rationing falters on human grounds because too many technical and marketing people get a taste of the future in building up the budget proposals and are reluctant to forego it in trimming back. The alternatives are shifting the project to a later period with a delayed introduction date, or partitioning the project, if feasible.

SPANNING BUDGET PERIODS

Once multiple time periods are considered, a distinction needs to be made between projects started in prior time periods, to be completed in the original budget period or later, and projects being newly initiated. Under conditions of budgetary constraint, an objective look at previously authorized projects is also warranted.

Besides the natural need to update benefit and cost forecasts, two factors need to be considered in older projects. First the hurdle rate may have changed since the project was first authorized. Higher management not only has a tendency to continuously tighten standards, but also may have different expectations of the future state of business, inflation, and interest rates from one period to the next. There is a built-in bias toward higher hurdle rates at the time of this writing; few managers in the author's experience are lowering hurdle rates with the fall since 1982 in inflation and interest rates. This tends to put even previously approved projects under scrutiny in each budget renewal period.

Offsetting this, particularly with regard to projects nearing completion, is the principle that sunk cost should be ignored in deciding whether to continue a project. All prior costs have already been incurred and, under accounting rules, have been expensed to prior-period profit and loss accounts. Only newly to be incurred costs should count in a decision to continue an older project into the current period. Assuming that reforecasting does not greatly change the benefit forecast, the decision to expend the limited remainder of R&D costs should greatly raise the profitability index for projects nearing completion. Thus, in multiperiod analysis, completing older projects tends to produce higher net present value for the firm than initiating new projects, excepting only those with the highest benefit-to-cost ratio. It should be noted that this principle also applies in preparing budget submittals in the first place. However, with reasonable availability of funds, all projects with a positive NPV at the hurdle rate would be accepted so that rank ordering is not required. In budget rationing, however, ignoring sunk costs is the correct procedure in deciding which projects to save.

The first inclination of the research manager when considering a multiperiod perspective with constraint in the current period is to defer to future periods the lowest benefit-to-cost ratio (BCR) projects that will not fit in the current budget limitation. A number of fallacies mar this approach. The lowest BCR project may not be the most postponable since its market window may be fixed by competition. Thus, deferment may so reduce the prospective benefits as to drop its BCR below acceptability in a future period. Although the lowest BCR projects make the smallest contribution to net present value, other projects may retain their BCR if postponed. It is even possible for the BCR to improve by postponement. For example, personal computer prices are falling steadily each year so that a project using one might be even more profitable in the subsequent budget period.

Quirin proposed a useful strategy for handling the postponing problem in multiperiod budget constraint (1967, p. 182). He constructed a postponability index in the following manner. For each project, the net present value should be calculated both for the next budget period and for the current one. The difference between the next period's net present value and the current one's represents the loss (or gain) from postponement. This divided by the project cost gives an index of postponability by comparing the net present value of losses or gains per dollar of funds made available by deferral. The index permits the project to be ranked, with those with the greatest loss ratio being selected for retention and those with gains or minimal relative losses being postponed until the budget limit is reached.

It should be noted that where the net present values are insensitive to when the project is done, such a procedure will provide no guidance because the differences and the index will be zero. This additional calculation, however, does assist in highlighting the projects for which postponement would be the equivalent of abandonment. Thus, it tends to retain projects that make a contribution to the net present value of the firm and that might otherwise be rejected under constraint by simple ranking procedure.

PARTITIONABLE LARGE PROJECTS

Some projects, such as a hydroelectric dam, are inherently unpartitionable and must be treated on a mutually exclusive basis. Others are so naturally partitionable that they may almost be treated as separate independent projects. Discretionary ability to partition characterizes a third group of projects. Neither technical nor marketing people seem to be able to escape being enmeshed in large, grandiose, interrelated schemes that, as usually presented, are unpartitionable.

The system architect is often unwilling to begin with less than a full system capable of being optimized in a technical sense as the design progresses. From the point of view of marketing, the incentive is to offer the fullest package possible for the high end of the market, while preserving the option of addressing the low-end commodity-priced portion of the market. Consider the following *hypothetical* example, chosen because the author is not now, nor ever has been, involved in such a product decision.

It is technically possible to design a word processor capable of being contained within the case of an electronic typewriter. In our hypothetical company, the two projects (high-end word processor and low-end electronic typewriter) may be treated as initially exclusive, as most of the industry does today, or as one partitionable project. In the absence of budget rationing, they may be justifiable as separate independent products/projects. With budget rationing, an alternative to considering them mutually exclusive is to consider partitioning. It is possible to construct an electronic typewriter with sufficient physical holes (empty spaces) and electronic "hooks" (access ports) so that the product may first be produced as an electronic typewriter, and later upgraded with word processor features: more internal memory, multiple line electronic display, small (3½ inch) floppy discs, and communications to larger systems and peripherals.

In designing such a system to be partitionable, the system's architect gives up some portion of optimization capability since interfaces between subsystems limit design flexibility to subsystem optimization only. Accommodation to the flexing of budgets, however, is only one of several advantages, which include feature flexibility, piecewise obsolescense, and so on.

Once partitioning is realizable, the core project must stand by itself for financial approval on the basis of its own benefit-to-cost ratio, and subsequent additions then become separate independent projects in the manner in which their approvals are handled. They become practical projects to replace the fictitious ones considered in mutually exclusive project evaluation.

SUMMARY AND CONCLUSION

Budget rationing is seen as a less-than-desirable situation as compared with accepting all projects at or above the hurdle return, which maximizes the net present value of future streams of income less current costs. It arises from internal reasons where top management does not wish to commit itself to new debt or equity, or from external reasons when the cost of raising external capital is excessive or capital funds are unobtainable because of the threat of insolvency.

The research manager's response to budget constraints should be to minimize its impact on the net present value of the R&D program. Ranking projects by return-to-cost or benefit-to-cost ratio is the immediately perceived solution, particularly for single-period, independent projects. In larger organizations, handling this analysis on a computer through linear programming assists in bringing in other financial and nonfinancial constraints.

Projects, however, may not be all independent. Mutually exclusive projects require the artifice of analyzing the fictitious project formed by the differences in their benefits and costs to determine whether the increment of the larger over the smaller is marginally justified.

Projects often overlap budget periods and must be separated into continuing and newly originated tasks. Continuing projects should be analyzed at the current year's hurdle rate, but should also be evaluated ignoring sunk costs from previous budget intervals. This tends to raise the priority of completing older projects so their benefit stream can commence.

While it is tempting for the research manager to defer to subsequent periods projects with lower benefit-to-cost ratios, the practice does not adequately reflect the potential losses or gains of deferment and their impact on net present value. Assessing the postponability index of projects is one tactic for shifting projects between time periods.

Large projects may be suitable for constructive partitioning to take them out of the mutually exclusive category and make the supplemental portions beyond the core project amenable to handling as separate independent and potentially postponable projects.

EXERCISES

1. Kappa Division (Tables 5.2 and 6.1) is facing a budget cutback which the general manager has indicated may be in one of four categories: $250,000; $500,000; $750,000; or $1,000,000. Prepare your proposed fall-back positions as to projects to be canceled or postponed. (Note: although Kappa used IRR, this may be converted to benefit-to-cost ratio, approximately, by using Figure 5.5).

2. Assume new relay controls and tele relay modifications are mutually exclusive projects. How does this change your answer to Exercise 1?

REFERENCES

Baker, N. R., W. E. Souder, C. R. Shumway, P. M. Maher and A. H. Rubenstein, "A Budget Allocation Model for Large Hierarchical R&D Organizations," *Management Science*, **23** (1): 59–70 (1976).

Bierman, Harold, Jr., and Seymour Smidt, *The Capital Budgeting Decision*, New York: Macmillan, 1975. *See* particularly Chapters 8 and 22.

Haynes, W. Warren, and William R. Henry, *Management Economics*, 3d ed., Dallas: Business Publications, 1974.

Quirin, G. David, *The Capital Expenditure Decision*, Homewood, IL: Irwin, 1967. *See* particularly Chapter 9.

Van Horne, James C., *Financial Management and Policy*, Englewood Cliffs, NJ: Prentice-Hall, 1974.

Weingartner, H. Martin, *Mathematical Programming and the Analysis of Capital Budgeting Problems*, Englewood Cliffs, NJ: Prentice-Hall, 1963.

10

A NOTE ON THE PUBLIC SECTOR

This book thus far has examined the techniques used by industrial research management for taking decisions in the competitive marketplace and raising funds in the competitive financial markets. Can any of these techniques for financial management be used effectively in the public sector?

It must be realized, initially, that there are two types of public institutions: public business undertakings, and publc social undertakings. The Tennessee Valley Authority is an example of the former. It is a business in all respects, except that the Congress decreed ownership should be by the federal government for the benefit of all citizens. It is not part of the purpose of these reflections on the public sector to pass judgment on this decision, but merely to note its impact. To the extent that a public business undertaking follows the principles of business financial management and reports a surplus, it is providing to its shareholders (the citizens) a return as would any commercial business. To the extent, however, that it does not follow such principles and does not create a surplus, it is in effect being used for a social purpose because it is then providing its customers with a good or service priced below market. In general, when a public agency is organized as a business and run for a business purpose, operating under the financial principles elaborated in previous chapters is natural and practical for public research management. It would certainly appear to be necessary in countries such as the United Kingdom where companies have been nationalized an denationalized according to which political party is in power. It is an approach to fairness in countries such as Canada and Australia where some markets have public companies competing with privately owned ones (e.g., Air Canada and CP Air).

Public social undertakings, however, have constituencies generally much larger than businesses because there are many indirect beneficiaries as well as users of a public agency's services. Also, many public products and services are not sold on a price basis, and those that are sold on a price basis, are often not priced in relation to cost, either average or marginal. Social benefits then are the value of all of these goods and services to all direct and indirect constituents. Social costs, on the other hand, may be either actual costs, as in a private business, or the opportunity cost to the public of the next most promising project that did not find its way into the public agency's budget. Transferring the financial principles in earlier chapters to the social side of the public sector may be elusive or even uncalculable. Even so, benefit/cost analysis is widely attempted in the public sector, subject to the imprecise nature of the calculations of intangible benefits and costs.

These notes on the public sector bear first on the appropriate discount rate to be used; multiple arguments exist for alternate methods of computation. Opportunity costs to the national economy are not the same as those for a private company. Some standards for social evaluation are reviewed subsequently, followed by a discussion of the relative importance of consumers' and producers' welfare.

DISCOUNT RATE IN THE PUBLIC SECTOR

The use of the internal rate of return in the public sector does not by itself demand calculation of a discount rate, but leaves open the question of what hurdle rate to choose. The other methods of project selection and evaluation, however, do depend on the use of a discount rate. While economists generally agree on weighted average (or marginal) cost of capital in the private case, there is more extensive argument in the case of the public sector. Several authors give the views of still other sources beyond those covered here (Quirin, 1967; Gibson, 1981).

At an earlier date, the present author also found the occasion to address the question of the appropriate discount rate (Ellis, 1979, pp. 168–170). Reflections on that analysis and other more recent views indicate that arguments about appropriate public sector discount rates and hurdle rates seem to fall into five identifiable classes: flow of funds; government cost of capital; private opportunity rate; social discount rate; and administrative fiat.

Flow of Funds

The flow-of-funds argument is essentially one of how mathematical models are influenced by discounting. If it is assumed that all benefits and costs are estimated in constant dollars, then one can argue that the proper discount rate should be the real rate of interest. The simple reason is because market interest rates set a premium over the real rate to allow for inflation (Sprinkel, 1971, pp. 214–215). However, since current dollar benefits should rise from the constant dollar estimates by the same inflationary factors, the inflation premiums in denominator and numerator should cancel, leaving only the real interest rate to count in discounting.

One study found the effects of technological change—the lowering of future costs and revenues—to be an additional discounting factor (Peck, 1974, p. 427). The author thus proposed the discount rate to be the sum of the real interest rate and the anticipated annual cost reduction due to technological change. This theoretical concept, however, was not supported when the model was tested against empirical data, which by an appreciable margin indicated a higher actual discount rate.

Still another author studied a growing public business undertaking (Manne, 1967, p. 41). He observed that if the business were not to be a burden on the central government, it would have to be self-financing, which required a return equal to or greater than the growth rate. Thus, the growth rate was considered to be an appropriate rate for discounting.

The discount rates in these three examples were set mechanistically according to the mathematical constraints of the models used, and they point up the problem of using theoretical abstractions in setting a discount rate. In addition, the real rate of interest, which was stable for many years prior to 1970, became negative during the hyperinflation of the 1970s, and in the 1980s has stubbornly remained at an appreciably higher level than its pre-1970 level of 3 to 4%.

Government Cost of Capital

Since government bodies are often regular issuers of bonds in financial markets, some authors argue for using the cost of money to the government agency as an independently set discount rate, a view that approximates the concept of the cost of capital to the private firm.

One important problem with this approach is that in the United States, interest on bonds of the federal government and its agencies is subject to federal income tax, whereas bonds of state and local governments are not, and consequently pay lower interest rates than on federal securities. One can question whether the desirability of a public sector research project should depend upon the tax status of the government agency that issues the securities to fund it.

Partially to get around this problem, another source suggests using the time value of money, defined as the interest rate of default-free securities—those issued by the federal government which has the power to print money to redeem them (Bierman and Smidt, 1975, pp. 179–183). A separate adjustment may be required for risk and uncertainty. Since local governments can default, as provided in the current bankruptcy act, their rate would be higher than the federal government's rather than lower, as would be the case were their tax status to effectively lower their borrowing rate. Since commercial firms subject to competition would discount at still higher rates owing to higher risks, this approach is quite consistent with the arguments presented earlier in Chapter 6.

An argument against this approach on social welfare grounds is that corporations currently pay income tax, which is a social benefit. Also corporate shareholders pay income tax on dividends. Thus, a dollar invested in a private business has a higher social benefit, at the same discount rate, than a dollar invested in the public sector.

Private Opportunity Rate

When a government runs a large deficit and borrows in the financial markets to cover it, it competes for funds with the private sector. In an economy with nearly full employment, government projects compete with private projects for staffing. Marginal analysis reveals that when a marginal government project is approved, its social cost is the displacement of the marginal private project. Thus, a conservative approach to public projects would insist that they produce a return equivalent to a private project, lest there be an economic loss to the society from accepting the public project (Quirin, 1967, pp. 152–155; Haynes and Henry, 1974, pp. 578–580).

Within this school of thought, multiple approaches have been devised to take into account the discriminatory implications of taxation discussed in earlier sections of this chapter. One approach suggests examining the tax structure to locate where revenue sources are to determine the marginal effect of a public project on the private sector.

Another approach is to consider the marginal cost of capital in the most productive private firms because this is where it would be most efficient for alternate employment to be created for the benefit of the economy as a whole.

The intellectually satisfying nature of this argument is based on the economic concept that public projects should not drive out private ones in a market-based economy. This is certainly fair for public business undertakings, but raises an arguable question of appropriateness for public social undertakings. In any case, approval of a public project at a discount rate lower than the private opportunity rate implies that some social value has supplanted an economic one in the public interest.

Social Discount Rate

A contrasting argument to that of the private opportunity rate is that all public projects are of social value, and that the discount rate, whether high or low, should be set as a value judgment and not in a sterile attempt to obtain a rate that has some theoretical economic meaning (Gibson, 1981, pp. 204–208). In opposition to market-based arguments are those that take into consideration the current historically high real interest rates and the difficulty of defining in economic terms projects in environmental protection , workplace safety, and so on; the socially regressive nature of market rates and the imperfect nature of benefit/cost analysis.

If the use of a social discount rate were to be broadly adopted, public business undertakings might underprice their services or products, and resources would be devoted increasingly to the public sector at the expense of the private sector. This shift has happened to some extent in the last 50 years in the United States and to a still greater degree in many other countries of the world. This raises still another question—since social benefits are also obviously a value judgment—as to whether the use of objective methods in the public sector has any intrinsic merit. There is a case that can be made for only making value judgments to establish social benefits, and then evaluating them with objectively established discount rates. This would allow a government agency, within its assigned social mission, to at least rank-order projects economically and to attempt to maximize the net present value of a research program that addresses social issues.

Administrative Fiat

The difficulties cited above in establishing a generally agreed-on criterion for public discount rates is often settled by administrative or legislative fiat. Of the two, the latter is preferable because representative legislative assemblies at least consider the views of the plural interest groups affected. Setting discount rates administratively raises the ancient Roman question, Who watches the custodian?

In the United States, the executive and legislative branches have been at odds over this subject during the years. The rate, set at 10% in 1972 (OMB Circular A-94), was subsequently reduced to 7% (OMB Circular A-104). However, for water resources, a rate of 6⅞% was later established (U.S. Water Resources Council, 1978). Such rates, well below private opportunity rates then prevailing, reflect strong value preferences for public, as opposed to private, projects.

The Intelsat Consortium was established as an intergovernmental body in 1965 (Snow, 1975). Although members were largely government agencies, a few foreign public corporations were represented on the governing board, and a federally chartered private corporation (Comsat) served as the United States operating agency. Following a consideration of alternatives, the required rate was set at 14% which was above the rates in effect for the various government agencies at the time, when expressed as borrowing rates in U.S. dollars, and above the weighted cost of capital for any of the foreign public corporations at that time. That it was then below Comsat Corporation's requested rate of return was primarily due to Comsat's overcapitalization at the time it went public. However, the 14% rate was well above Comsat's opportunity cost since its enabling act only allowed external investment in U. S. Treasury securities at a much lower rate. Thus, the choice of an above-market rate for the Intelsat Consortium perhaps reflected a view that international communications should provide high returns to the various nations rather than merely serve as a socially supported activity.

Reprise: Public Discount Rate

As the discussion above shows, there is no agreement on the one best way to establish a public discount rate. The public sector research manager should welcome a rate set by some higher administrative or legislative authority, whatever may have been the reasoning, because it at least makes it possible to accomplish the agency's assigned task: establishing an optimal portfolio of projects that maximizes the net present value of the program, within the constraints of budget limitations, and achieves the assigned social or business purpose of the government agency (Baker et al., 1976).

Much more difficult then is the task of a research manager in the public sector who must justify also the hurdle rate assigned to the R&D program. In the absence of a social or political cause guiding selection of a lower rate, the arguments presented earlier in this chapter suggest using a rate that reflects the supporting agencies' cost of capital and the opportunity rate in the private sector.

Once a discount rate has been selected and approved, financial managers of research in the public sector can logically follow methods outlined in this book for the private sector, after giving due weight to differing concepts of opportunity costs, evaluation standards, and welfare considerations resulting from broader sector constituencies.

OPPORTUNITY COSTS TO THE ECONOMY

Various motivations exist to undertake research in the public sector (Gibson, 1981, pp. 180–182). Some research directly benefits users of directly related goods and services. Most research has indirect beneficiaries in the citizenry at large. Opportunity costs to the economy may be looked at as the costs of private projects displaced, as in the previous discussion of the private opportunity rate. They may also be looked at from the viewpoint of what is foregone if the project is not undertaken.

A clear example is the means of providing citizen safety, ranging form local police protection to national defense. The cost of research on advanced weapons systems can be measured against the opportunity cost to the public if the armed forces are not properly prepared. Law enforcement R&D expenses may be measured against the opportunity cost to the public of increased crime. These tradeoffs are intended only to demonstrate that opportunity cost has its counterpart in the public sector as well as in industrial research.

Thus, the concept of social benefit from public sector reseach includes not only direct and indirect benefits, but also direct and indirect costs avoided by the nation's citizens.

The concept of opportunity cost substantially justifies the federal government's assumption of the major share of basic research in the United States. Business would be forced to do more basic research if government did not support it, or to license the research from other nations as Japan has done so effectively. Both expedients are capable of quantification. Private companies would also be forced to contribute more for the education of skilled personnel if their training were not assisted by government grants to academia, and again this is quantifiable. When assessing net benefits, value judgments are made in determining how much is to be saved, not in recognizing that the concept of opportunity cost exists.

Very few governmental research and development activities are actually focused on economic tasks, although the ones that are can most easily be quantified as to benefits. "Free" services become more difficult to quantify, although methods have been proposed to attempt to do so (Haynes and Henry, 1974, pp. 564–576).

Public budget approvals are an intensely political process. The public sector R&D manager must recognize this and be prepared to defend his budget with quantified estimates of benefits and costs, no matter how imprecise and intangible calculations of such things as opportunity costs may be. The political process is unlikely to accept all benefit computations set forward and may reject or modify many items. A high priority must thus be given to a careful compilation of third-party benefits that can be attributed to the research and that can be measured in terms of both positive returns and cost avoidance.

A public sector research organization in South America, the *Fundacion Chile*, is endowed jointly by the Chilean government and the ITT Corporation. A unified criterion was considered necessary by its board of directors to evaluate benefits for competing sectors of the economy. After a study by the foundation's economic director, a single benefit criterion was proposed and agreed on to assess the positive impact of each project on the gross domestic product of Chile (Adriasola, 1976).

STANDARDS FOR SOCIAL EVALUATION

Any social system has a natural tendency to self-optimize. Thus, a business considers its own benefits and costs. Many lesser agencies in government have a tendency to do the same. For the higher levels of government, there is a need to optimize on the national or state level. This involves considering social benefits of users and third parties, both on a positive return and opportunity cost basis.

Equally, upper levels of government should consider true social cost, not budgetary cost. The latter is one component of cost, but so are costs incurred by business and citizens as a result of government action. For example, if a research project requires that businesses collect and report additional data, that cost, although not paid by government, should be considered part of the social cost of government.

In the United States, the benefit-to-cost ratio method was imposed for information gathering by the Rivers and Harbors Act of 1902, and was extended as a project selection rule by the Flood Control Act of 1936 (provided that it did not adversely affect people's lives and security). It thus became widely accepted at all levels of government as the principle economic method. Projects should be accepted if, and only if, all social benefits discounted at the decreed rate divided by all social costs discounted at the same rate have a benefit-to-cost ratio greater than 1.0.

The economic director of the *Fundacion Chile* proposed similar rule to its board of directors, namely that the ratio of the positive impact of each project on the gross domestic product of Chile divided by the project's cost to the foundation be greater than 1.0. As part of this cost, social costs of others were factored in to reduce the benefit impact. The board approved this concept subject to budget limitations and subject to a social exception if agreed to by the board (Adriasola, 1979).

In contrast to these largely objective approaches (with subjective exceptions possible), mere value judgments form the basis of the work of many levels of government. Medical researchers, for example, tend to avoid objective criteria because this means putting a dollar value on a human life. Agricultural, food, marine, and physical research in the public sector, however, tend to be amenable to objective analysis with the methods explained in earlier chapters. The public sector research manager should be prepared for increasing scrutiny of departmental research budgets on an objective basis and should relegate subjectivity and purely social evaluations to areas where they can be defended in terms of the inherent incalculability of the benefits in question.

PRODUCERS' VERSUS CONSUMERS' WELFARE

So far in this chapter the term *social welfare* has been used without differentiating society into producers and consumers. It may be argued that in the long run the well-being of consumers and of producers are so intertwined as to make this distinction moot. Research programs have to be put forward in the short run, however, and demand-side (pro-consumer) and supply-side (pro-producer) advocates abound. In developing countries, a different focus is necessary.

The basic equation for a national economy is that what is consumed plus what is invested (capital goods) plus what is exported have to be produced or imported. This rule applies to the total of goods and services. Where exports and imports nearly balance, production and consumption differ only by investment, which is a small percentage of GNP in the United States. Investment represents provision for future production and consumption, plus goods used in the provision of services. Thus, it cannot be zero, or there is neither growth nor replacement. On the other hand, it cannot grow too large, or the citizens will complain that their standard of living is being unduly restrained. Thus, in the developed economy where imports and exports nearly balance, producers' welfare and consumers' welfare are tightly interlocked, and it is fair to use either or both in estimating social benefits for public R&D programs, subject to the current political winds on the demand side or supply side.

In most developing countries, and from time to time in some developed ones, imports and exports are not in balance, with the excess of imports being funded by borrowing in world financial markets. In such countries, attempts to improve the welfare of producers by lowering imports or increasing exports tend to be made at the expense of consumers. Alternatively, attempts to rapidly improve the welfare of consumers usually come at the expense of producers, or cause large surges of imports and foreign borrowing. A practical solution for research programs is to bring into the social benefit and social cost estimates the impact of the research on each of the five terms of the economic equation.

SUMMARY AND CONCLUSION

This brief note on the public sector showed that the financial methods of industrial research management may be used also on public research programs with a number of special considerations. Public business undertakings can use these methods with minimal alteration. Public social undertakings, however, must measure also indirect benefits and costs to the economy as a whole lest the government agency suboptimize its activity.

Many arguments have been proposed for various discount rates in the public sector. In the end, however, administrative or legislative fiat may set the rates to be used by public sector research management. When this is not done, the research manager must choose one of several approaches: flow of funds, social discount rate, government cost of capital, and private opportunity rate. Some combination of the latter two has the greatest financial legitimacy.

Opportunity cost in the economy has its parallels in the public sector since potential research programs not only have direct and indirect benefits but also permit certain costs to be avoided.

Standards for social evaluation in the United States are set legislatively and administratively around the benefit-to-cost ratio. The research manager must be prepared for this quantitative scrutiny although in many fields the benefits are more subject to subjective value judgments than to objective measurements. The maximization of social benefits must give due weight to both consumers' and producers' welfare and the nature of their interaction in the national economy.

Having briefly touched on the special circumstances of the public sector, it is possible to answer affirmatively that private sector financial management techniques can be used effectively by pubic sector research managers within the limitations detailed in this chapter. Since the intended focus of this book is industrial research management, the public sector will be left at this point, and the private sector viewpoint reasserted in the final chapter.

REFERENCES

Adriasola, Luis, presentations to the board of directors of *Fundacion Chile,* Santiago, Chile, 1976–1979, while the author was a board member.

Baker, N. R., W. E. Souder, C. R. Shumway, P. M. Maher, and A. H. Rubenstein, "A Budget Allocation Model for Large Hierarchical R&D Organizations", *Management Science,* **23**(1): 59–70 (1976).

Bierman, Harold, Jr., and Seymour Smidt, *The Capital Budgeting Decision,* 4th ed., New York: Macmillan, 1975.

Ellis, Lynn W., "Economies of Scale in Telecommunications: Analysis, Strategies, Management," doctoral dissertation, Pace University, New York, 1978, and Ann Arbor, MI: University Microfilms, 1979.

Fleisher, Gerald A., *Capital Allocation Theory,* New York: Appleton-Century-Crofts, 1969.

Gibson, John E., *Managing Research and Development,* New York: Wiley, 1981, *See* particularly Chapter 7.

Haynes, W. Warren, and William R. Henry, *Managerial Economics*, 3rd ed., Dallas: Business Publications, 1974.

Manne, A. S., ed., *Investment for Capacity Expansion*, Cambridge, MA: M.I.T. Press, and London: Allen & Irwin, 1967.

Office of Management and Budget (OMB), *Discount Rates to be Used in Evaluating Time Distributed Costs and Benefits*, Circular no. A-94, Washington: March 27, 1972, amended by, Circular no. A-104

Peck, Stephen C., "Alternative Investment Models for Firms in the Electric Utilities Industry," *Bell Journal of Economics and Management Science*, 5(2): 420–458 (1974).

Quirin, G. David, *The Capital Expenditure Decision*, Homewood, IL: Irwin, 1967.

Snow, Marcellus S., "Investment Cost Minimization for Communications Satellite Capacity: Refinement and Application of the Chenery-Manne-Srinivasan Model," *Bell Journal of Economics*, 6(2): 621–643 (1975).

Sprinkel, Beryl Wayne, *Money & Markets: A Monetarist View*, Homewood, IL: Irwin, 1971.

U. S. Water Resources Council, "Principles and Standards for Planning Water and Related Land Sources," *Federal Register* 43-209, October 27, 1978; *Federal Register*, 43-210, October 30, 1978.

11

A SUMMING UP

Practicing research managers have four dimensions to their work to which they must respond. This book has addressed only the financial dimension, which must now be readdressed in the context of the total research and development management task.

Though not part of the financial side of industrial research management, the other three dimensions are critically affected by financial considerations and therefore deserve comment, although a full analysis is not practical in a single chapter nor attempted here. The technological dimension of the research manager's work is also the operational task of managing the technological interface, which should occupy a prominent share of the research manager's working time. Similarly, the human resources dimension is also the operational task of managing people. Managing people and technology are each equally important in the typical research department, and together should be allocated 80% or more of the research manager's time.

The fourth dimension is not an operational task, but a necessary reaction to reality. We live in a world of large institutions, and it has been known since the writings of Machiavelli (1469–1527) that such institutions are subject to the influence of politics. In moving up to the managerial level, the research manager moves into the realm of politics and must learn to live in a political environment. But politics and finance, which represent the upward and sideways communications of the manager, should together not take more than 20% of the research manager's time in a well-managed corporation.

THE FINANCIAL DIMENSION REVISITED

In revisiting the financial side of industrial research management, as compared with the total task, one realizes that while this side is important to management, it is only one of the four dimensions with which the research manager must cope. Not only is the financial side important to proper research management, but also it is the language of communications to those superior levels of management that control the supply of money.

However, reliance on financial measures of performance does not alone ensure success. Financial measures do not give an early warning of impending technological change, which may be critical for business survival. Also their application may mask human resource problem if insufficient attention is given to retaining an adequately competent technical staff. Thus, the research manager must consider financial methods as only tools with which to defend research expenditures in a financial and political environment, rather than as a complete means to fulfillment of the overall research management task.

The first of these tools is microeconomics. Because of the time value of money, all research decisions need to be discounted in both benefits and costs to present monetary units for comparison. Thus, the further into the future benefits occur, the greater they must be to exceed research and start-up costs when discounted. Resources are always scarce and must be looked at both on an opportunity cost basis and in terms of marginal analysis. This leads to ranking projects by benefit-to-cost ratio or by some other equivalent scale to arrive at an optimum level of expenditure on projects with the greatest contribution to the net present value of the firm.

One financial dimension of the research manager's task lies within the financial accounting of overheads in a given budget year. Project cost accounting, however, requires running the research department on an internal direct costs plus overheads basis. The internal overheads must reflect fringes and times individuals are paid but do not work, plus the cost of supervision, support, and interfaces with other departments. In the budget dimension, the research manager's task is to plan, budget, organize, measure, and control overheads to their lowest realizable level.

The other axis of R&D projects is the time dimension through the R&D and product life cycles. R&D cycles start at a low level of certainty and increase to a satisfactory level, or projects are terminated. Products once introduced grow and mature, and then must be extended or replaced. The correct return must be obtained from this combined cycle, or the project is not worth doing. Since costs increase rapidly along the two cycles, early recognition and termination of unworthy projects is a key to having resources available to dedicate to potential winners.

The fourth financial tool available to the research manager is objective methods of project selection and evaluation which offset the problems and excuses of subjectivity. Of the objective methods, internal rate of return is offered as a good tool and easy to use with computer technology. As a criterion for evaluation, the company's weighted cost of capital matches other financial assessment criteria, when the relative risk of R&D projects is considered.

Objective measurements of risk are another modification of project selection and evaluation methods. Probabilistic methods of evaluation of technical and commercial risks are useful where the number of projects and their probability of random outcomes are both sufficiently large. A related technique is to apply a premium over the weighted cost of capital to account for the degree of risk. General management's tendency to be risk averse is largely offset by the portfolio effect wherein a large number of R&D projects lower overall risk. When the outcomes are nonprobabilistic, game theory approaches may be necessary to deal with uncertainty.

Achieving results in the application of objective analysis requires measurement in two areas: budgets and projects. Budget measurements focus on deviations in spending and in applied time, and need to be fed back promptly for effectiveness in management. Project measurements of past performance give a basis for risk analysis and estimating. Above all, objectives need to be set both challengingly and realistically. These measurements act as controls by highlighting for different levels of management where the plan is not being followed. Complete perfection of measurement and control will not, however, offset faulty strategies or poor project selection.

The combination of projects selected, discretionary activities, support, interfaces, and supervision leads to an overall budget and to the question, How much should be spent on R&D? Objective answers come from investment theory, zero base budgeting, and a number of optimization models. Optimization based on maximizing current earnings tends to forget the investment nature of R&D, whereas maximizing the impact of R&D on the price of the company's shares is an approach comparable to that of investment theory. A research manager may have to use elements of a number of these approaches in determining the level of budget proposals to be submitted and in defending them before higher management.

All too often, the R&D manager must live with an approved budget lower than originally submitted for reasons internal to the firm or because it becomes difficult to raise funds externally. Strategies are then needed for pruning back to the best set of projects that will fit into the constrained budget. Initially this may be looked at just from a single time period, but consideration must also be given to projects that span budget periods and to handling mutually exclusive opportunities.

These then are the eight sets of financial management tools available to the research manager in an industrial corporation:

Microeconomics
Department budgeting
Project and product cycles and costs
Project selection and evaluation methods
Treatment of risk and uncertainty
Measurement and control
Budget optimization
Budget rationing

Extension of this financial approach to the public sector requires adapting to other considerations. Costs of capital differ in the public sector. Opportunity costs in the economy have a social dimension. Value judgments enter into determining social benefits and social costs. and also into setting discount rates. Consumers' welfare may differ from that of producers in determining social welfare. Even so, many of the financial tools of research management used in the private sector have application also to public research projects.

The underlying message to the research manager is that reluctance to quantify financially is no longer acceptable in the modern financially oriented world. A need exists to know and understand the financial side of research management and to be comfortable in using quantified financial answers in the sometimes difficult task of communicating between the technical sector and higher management.

At the same time, the research manager must realize the impact on the inherently long time cycles of R&D activity of using only financial yardsticks which, because of discounting, are inherently short-term oriented. The business world is a fast-changing mix of realities of the technological and market environments and of the strategic reactions of competitors to these environments. Not all of these realities fall into the neat models of microeconomics and finance. If they did, a business world peopled only by bankers and other finance people might suffice. In the real world, however, there is a need for insight into the nonfinancial aspects of technology and of people which must not be lost sight of in the management of industrial research.

EXPLOITING NEW TECHNOLOGY

One of the principal areas in which the economic and financial models fail is in their assumption of continuity. Yet so many examples abound of discontinuities in technology dramatically affecting the survival of businesses that one author called this the "age of discontinuity" (Drucker, 1968). So prevalent now are these discontinuities that this author prefers to use the term *age of obsolescence,* or *shadow of obsolescence* (Levitt, 1975).

Mathematical models of the deterministic type used earlier in this book and in many of the sources cited do not produce their neat results if subjected to discontinuity. Internal rate of return calculations may be multiple valued under such conditions (Quirin, 1967, pp. 49–57). Extended mathematical series may not converge, or may need to include higher-order terms, which complicates their application.

Even more important, however, than the technical difficulties of mathematical modeling under conditions of discontinuity is the nature of the technological change itself. The research manager may wish to consider the frame of mind of the hypothetical research directors at some earlier established companies at similar points of discontinuity:

Buggy whip manufacturers at the introduction of the horseless carriage

Soap manufacturers on learning of detergents

Silk worm growers and rayon manufacturers on hearing of DuPont's nylon

DuPont on hearing of Celanese's polyester

Tire manufacturers on learning of Michelin's radial tires

Vacuum tube manufacturers when Bell Labs' scientists invented the transistor

These discontinuities, and many others not cited, did two things. First, they substituted for an existing product, and second, they changed radically the nature of the market. It was not that the established companies did not have a good product, low production costs, and good customer relations, but rather that they had an investment in the past with which they were reluctant to part. Regrettably, the use of increasingly sophisticated financial tools will probably make it even more difficult to discard the past by permitting the argument that earlier investments have yet to be paid back. What this approach fails to understand is that the customer will desert the older product anyway, and the payback will never happen. To be effective in the exploitation of technical change, the research manager must understand, or have people who understand, when to abandon older technology (Foster, 1983). This most always means having a listening watch on new science, from whence comes discontinuity, to know early enough to be effective because by the time a competitor introduces a new technology, it is often too late to react.

Equally important to understanding new science is understanding where old science cannot go. A clear warning of impending discontinuity is when an older technology becomes increasingly difficult to improve. Business line after business line, from cash registers to telephone central offices to wrist watches, has seen this happen, with older mechanical products succumbing to new electronic ones.

Strategic analysis of competitor reactions to reality is an important part of understanding competitive technological threats. Watching only current competitors, however, is not enough since most market share gains at points of discontinuity are made by new competitors unencumbered by the heritage of past technology to cloud their vision and able to move quickly to exploit a new opportunity.

The critical point for a company is the time when the potential of new technology has become apparent. Funds must be cut back on the older technology and rapidly invested in the new technology, in skilled people to develop it, and in facilities to produce it. All of this occurs at a time when certainty is low and benefit and cost estimates are of high risk, which is the antithesis of the financially objective methods treated in this book. Yet not to mount the attack quickly gives the new entrepreneurs a head start from which to proceed farther and faster down the learning curve in the new technology.

An equally flawed strategy is to defend the old technology in a high-end approach—features, size, and so on—while letting the new technology start in the low-end commodity-priced sector of the market. IBM followed this approach in minicomputers, letting Digital Equipment Corporation's minis become a major market force. IBM has since learned its lesson and is now in the fray in personal computers and small business systems. General Motors, Ford, and Xerox all have cause to regret the market position left by this strategy to Japanese competitors.

As shown in Chapter 4, the transition in the product life cycle to rapid growth is abrupt. Then, there is not time to see and react to prevent a substantial market share loss. Financial measures are not too helpful there also, particularly for the larger firms. As those marginal firms in the older technology fold their production facilities under the impact of new competitors, large firms often gain apparent market share for a while (e.g., RCA in vacuum tubes and Lever in soap)—apparent, that is, because the inward look often sees only the older technology and not the true total market of old and new.

Finally, survival under conditions of technical discontinuity requires a personal rapport between the research director and the chief executive or general manager. The financial measures for communication ar inadequate in such instances, and if the higher manager's philosophy only trusts the financial approach, decisions are unlikely to be taken in a timely manner, but are likely to be delayed until the crisis becomes obvious, which is of course too late.

Unfortunately, only one chief executive officer out of five in U.S. business includes the senior technical officer as part of the inner circle of management (Foster, 1983). In this author's experience, the level of true rapport between general and research managers at lower levels, such as divisions, is probably not much higher. In many cases, it is not in the professional nature of research managers to work toward establishing such a rapport; they consider it "politics." Yet it is precisely when more objective measures are not adequate to the task that such a close working relationship and mutual trust is most necessary, or the tactics of political confrontation may need to be employed for the research manager to get across the critical nature of the discontinuity.

HUMAN RESOURCES MANAGEMENT

The management of technical people and the financial managment of research and development have of necessity partially conflicting objectives. Much has been written elsewhere on the management of technical people from the beginning level (Gray, 1979) through intermediate levels (Gibson, 1981) to the matrix management level (Cleland, 1983). Common to most of these sources is the idea that engineers produce best in unstructured environments, under wide limits of self-control and with opportunities for growth. In many technical specialties, engineers are scarce, independent, and mobile between employers.

Financial management methods are structured, and when well-applied provide prompt feedback that limits the degree of self-control by individuals. The realities of the ups and downs of the business cycle lead many general managers to flex R&D budgets up and down with the business cycle to preserve short-term profits.

The research manager must live between these two conflicting philosophies in a balanced manner, in the sense of being efficient and being human (Herzberg, 1976). Both the need to be efficient and, often, the personal reward (bonus) structure cause the research manager to view the technical activity financially. Yet the necessity of hiring, training, and retaining a competent technical staff leads to a basic conflict between full manpower flexibility and business fluctuations.

In many technologies in recent years, and particulary in electronics, a new strategic reality has become apparent—Japanese managements take the longer-term view and let profits fluctuate with the business cycle rather than people (Pascale and Athos, 1981). Thus, many U.S. R&D departments, with projects deferred through the trough of the business cycle, have found their Japanese competitors have proceeded at full pace during the same period and have beaten them to the market with new products.

Here again is a threatening competitive situation in whch rapport and mutual trust between general and technical managers are needed to establish a technical investment strategy capable of reconciling the opposing forces of people and of profits on a monthly or quarterly reporting basis.

THE POLITICAL REALITY

Just as the technical and personnel realities modify the application of financial methods to research management, so does the political reality of the business organization. The management team of the basic business unit is composed of representatives of many diverse functions: marketing, personnel, manufacturing, technical, and quality control, as well as finance. When any one discipline begins to dominate excessively in decision making, there is a strong likelihood of a coalition forming among the other functions to redress the balance somewhat. Politics has been defined as the art of the possible. The possible in business organization is sufficient balance between the opposing functions to enable the functioning of management as a team—as a viable subsystem within the industrial system in which it operates.

It must be remembered that each function in the basic business organization is a center of power in its own right. Thus, each must operate in a manner in which it contributes to the whole operation. The withdrawal by any power center of support to another creates a condition of conflict that cannot be ignored by general management. Thus, each functional head has at least the level of control over other functions that may be termed *management by veto*.

The typical research manager is far more of a professional person than a politician and in this author's experience is less likely to use the tactics of politics against other functional heads than they are to use them against the technical function. It is often a shock to the research manager, for example, when the quality manager holds up the release of a new product as a means for pressing for a change in the behavior of the technical department, or marketing, or manufacturing.

The extent to which a research manager uses power politics in a business organization is a matter of individual preference. It must be recognized that the general manager cannot permit too much trifling with line authority or too much conflict between functional heads. Thus, excessive politics may put the research manager's job on the line.

There are, however, two instances in which the research manager should exercise the full power of politics. The first is at the moment he perceives that technical discontinuity threatens the survival of the business. Rarely can any other functional head or the general manager see this clearly. As custodian of the technical strength of the division or company, the R&D director has an obligation to sound an early warning of impending danger.

The conflict such an action will cause may be considerable. Manufacturing and financial directors may feel threatened and react accordingly. It must also be remembered that there is an ancient tradition of disposing of the messenger who bears bad news. But if the business does not survive the discontinuity, the research manager's job is likely to be disposed of anyway.

A second instance when the research manager should exercise the power of politics is when there is that rare clear agreement with another functional head (usually marketing) that some specific technical activity needs to be undertaken for the good of the company even if the financial analysis does not support it. The same strong subjective reaction from two different functional heads usually means that something has been overlooked in the preparation of the project evaluation. The need for discretionary projects was covered previously in Chapter 5. It may take politics from time to time to permit the initiation of such projects when the financial analysis does not support them at the outset.

The political dimension of the research manager's job is thus the means by which action may be obtained in the technical or personnel dimensions when not objectively supported by the financial side of research management. Its sparing use to temper financial objectivity will help retain the research manager's creditability as a cooperative member of the management team.

REFERENCES

Cleland, David I., ed., *Matrix Management Systems Handbook*, New York: Van Nostrand Reinhold, 1983.

Drucker, Peter F., *The Age of Discontinuity*, New York: Harper & Row, 1968.

Foster, Richard N., "To Exploit New Technology, Know When to Junk the Old," *New York Times*, **CCI**(85): 30 (May 2, 1983).

Gibson, John E., *Managing Research and Development*, New York: Wiley, 1981.

Gray, Irwin, *The Engineer in Transition to Management*, New York: IEEE Press, 1979.

Herzberg, Frederick, *The Managerial Choice: To Be Efficient and to Be Human*, Homewood, IL: Irwin, 1976.

Levitt, Theodore, "Marketing Myopia," *Harvard Business Review*, **53**(5): 26–48 (1975).

Pascale, Richard Tanner, and Anthony G. Athos, *The Art of Japanese Management*, New York: Simon & Schuster, 1981.

Quirin, G. David, *The Capital Expenditure Decision*, Homewood, IL: Irwin, 1967.

ANSWERS TO EXERCISES

Chapter 2

1. A parabola has the following equation:
    $y = a x^2 + b x + c$, where y = benefits/sales and
    $\qquad\qquad\qquad\qquad\qquad$ x = R&D/sales
    When $x = 0$, $y = 3$, so $c = y = 3$
    A parabola's slope is $2 a x + b$. When $x = 0$, slope $= 0.5$, so
    b = slope $= 0.5$. For each year, the value of x when $y = 0$ can
    be determined from Table 1.1 by dividing margin by sales ($\bar{x}$).
    Thus, $0 = a \bar{x}^2 + 0.5 \bar{x} + 3$, and $a = -0.5/\bar{x} - 3/(\bar{x})^2$. Optimum
    (x^*) occurs at zero slope. Thus $x^* = -0.5/2$ a.

Year	1975	1976	1977	1978	1979	1980
x	5	6.4	5.8	5.3	4.8	4.7
$\bar{x}$	15	15	15.3	15.8	16.6	16.6
a	-0.0467	-0.0467	-0.0455	-0.0437	-0.0410	-0.0410
optimum %	5.4	5.4	5.5	5.7	6.1	6.1
over (under)	(0.4)	1.0	0.3	(0.4)	(1.3)	(1.4)

2. IRR from Table 1.1 is 30.1%
    If two more years at 0.7/year, IRR is 48.7%.
    If 1981 is 0.5 and 1982 is 0.1%, IRR is 40.6%.

3. IRRs are 65.4%, 81.7% and 74.7%, respectively.

Chapter 3

1. Software applied time may be calculated as follows:

	Applied Days
2 Supervisors	234
4 Senior engineers	896
6 Junior engineers	1344
	2474

    This is 24.757% of the total applied days, and common services
    such as manager, secretarial, and allocations should be spilt ac-
    cordingly. The software budget is then as follows:

	Budget	Applied
Manager/secretarial	21,044	
Supervisors	80,000	36,000

Senior engineers	132,000	113,723
Junior engineers	144,000	124,062
Subtotal	377,044	
Fringes (35%)	131,965	
Spending (incl. Compr.)	193,699	
Allocation	50,010	
Total	757,718	273,785

The new overhead rate is $100 \times \dfrac{757,718 - 273,785}{273,785} = 176.76\%$

Software category A rate $= 2.7676 \times \dfrac{149,723}{1,130} = \$366.70/\text{day}$

Software category B rate $= 2.7676 \times \dfrac{124,062}{1,344} = \$255.47/\text{day}$

Similar calculations for hardware give 131.24%; $306.39/day; and $187.80/day for overhead, A and B rates, respectively.

Chapter 8

1. In Chapter 2 we found benefits (earnings) to sales as follows:
    $y = a x^2 + 0.5 x + 3$, where a varied by year as given in the answer to Exercise 1 of Chapter 2. Sales price/sales $(z) =$ price/earnings $\times$ earnings/sales (y),
    $z = (3 + 3 x)(a x^2 + 0.5 x + 3)$
    $= 3 a x^3 + (3a + 1.5) x^2 + 10.5 x + 9$
    Differentiating and setting equal to zero to find a maximum:
    $0 = 9 a x^2 + (6a + 3) x + 10.5$

For 1975 and 1976:
$0 = 0.4203 x^2 - 2.7198 x - 10.5$

$x_{\text{max}} = 6.84\%$ since only the positive root has economic meaning. This is 37% higher than actual R&D/sales and 27% higher than the optimum calculated on an earnings basis only for 1975, and 7% higher than the peak actual R&D/sales year of 1976. Gamma was clearly risk averse compared to that which would be expected of a public company. Subsequent years are left to the reader to calculate.

Chapter 9

1. Using Figure 5.5, and Table 5.2, the net present values of the eight lowest IRR projects may be calculated as (BCR − 1) times development cost:

	Net Present Value ($,000)
New relay control	950
New solid state (ss) relay	505
Telerelay modification	480
Relay modification	60
Silver relay	70
Gravity relay	350
Gold relay	110
Reed relay	1100

   a. $250,000 cutback choices:
       Cut telerelay, or   480
       Cut gravity relay   350 preferred

   b. $500,000 cutback choices:
       Cut s.s. relay, or   505 preferred
       Cut tele, silver, and relay mod.   610

   c. $750,000 cutback choices:
       Cut ss, gravity, and relay mod.   915 preferred
       Cut new relay control   950

   d. $1 million cutback choices:
       Cut new relay ctrl and mod.   1010 preferred
       Cut ss, tele, silver, & mod.   1115

2. The difference between the relay control and telerelay projects is $458,000 in cost, with a net present value difference of $470,000, for a benefit-to-cost ratio of 1.03 and an IRR of only a few percent. Thus, the new relay control should be canceled for the $500,000 and $750,000 cutback levels instead of the projects indicated in 1b and 1c above.

AUTHOR INDEX

SUBJECT INDEX

social, 170, 178
Western Electric Company, 75

Zero based budgeting, *see* Budget, zero base